...and then he's not

reflections on loss, mourning, mortality

Bryan Fox, Son

2019

Death doesn't always announce its impending arrival. In retrospect, anything could have been a warning sign. In retrospect, some things should have been. But there were books to read, series to binge, Facebook posts to Like.

So many things seem so important until something important happens.

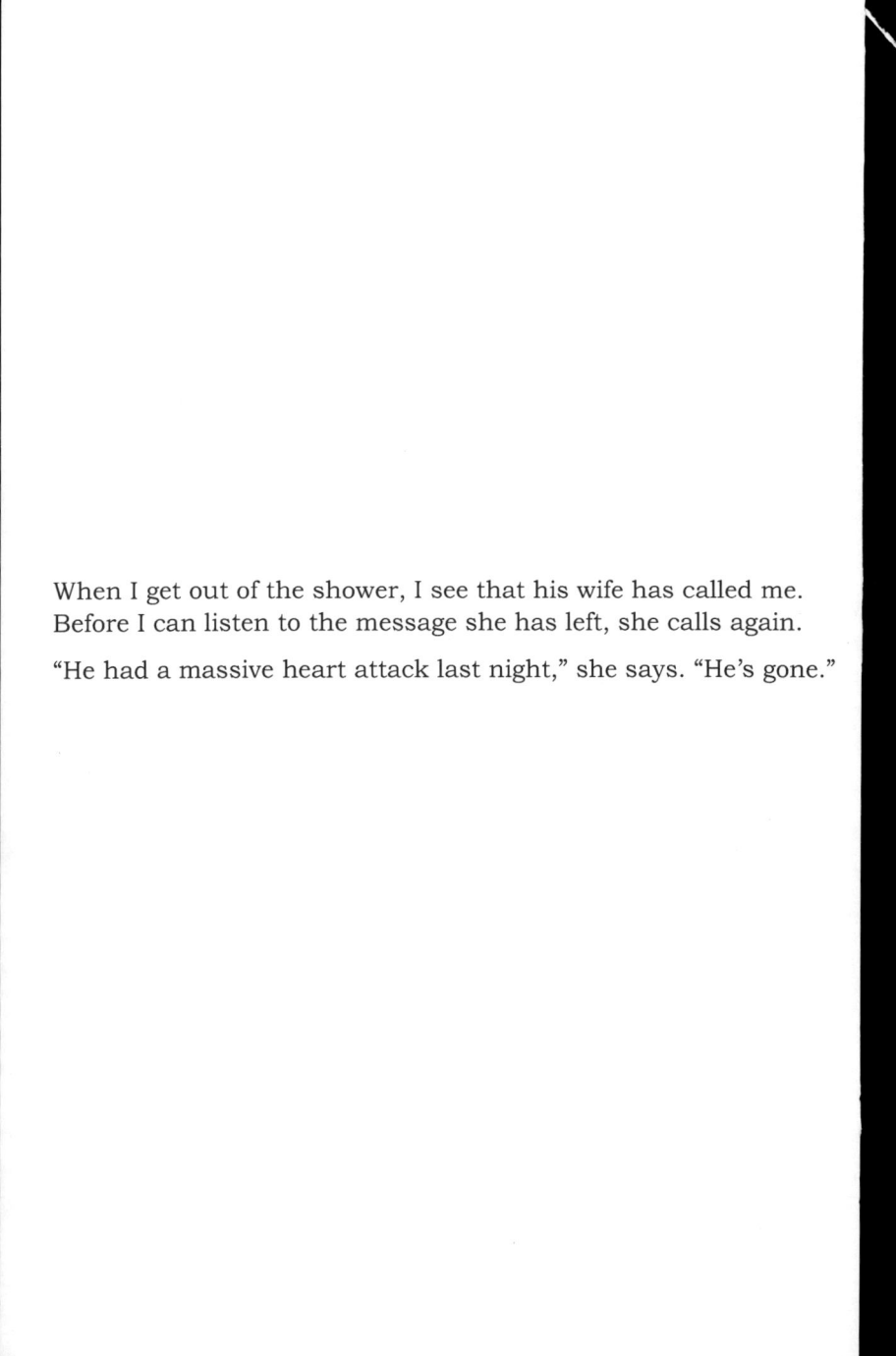

When I get out of the shower, I see that his wife has called me. Before I can listen to the message she has left, she calls again.

"He had a massive heart attack last night," she says. "He's gone."

Posterity will note that I did not drop the phone upon hearing the news. I did not scream "Why!" or pull at my hair. I did not push back against the nearest wall for support.

In fact, one hour after being informed of his death, I teach a class. It is a 4.5-hour class, and I do not mention what has just happened to the students. I want, perhaps, to exist for one more day in the normal world, this now liminal space of him existing.

I am not in denial.

I have not yet even begun to contemplate what his death is or what it means to me.

I text the news to a friend later that day, an old friend who I see infrequently but maintain a strong bond with, even in our general absence from each other's respective lives. Immediately, a call comes from her which I do not answer.

"No," I text back. "Not ready for that yet."

There is a moment, when you stub your toe, or bump your head on an open cabinet door, or cut yourself with a knife while preparing food, between the realization of what has happened and the onset of the pain. This moment, with regard to the news of his death, lasts nearly 10 hours, until I am home from work, in my room, sitting on my bed. It lasts until I open my laptop and begin to write his eulogy.

I do not know where to begin. I do not know how to continue. It is the most uncomfortable homework assignment ever, and it is due in less than 48 hours. It becomes hard to see the illuminated screen through the tears. It seems cliché to say one is "choking" on them, but that is, in fact, what it feels like.

This makes no sense. Clearly this is not possible. Clearly I misunderstood his wife. I talked to him 15 hours ago. I am going to meet him next weekend, to go to my storage unit out in NJ and take out some paintings to hang on the walls of my apartment.

I have tickets, two tickets, for a Yankees playoff game next week. That's his birthday gift. We literally just talked about this.

He was right there.

And now he isn't.

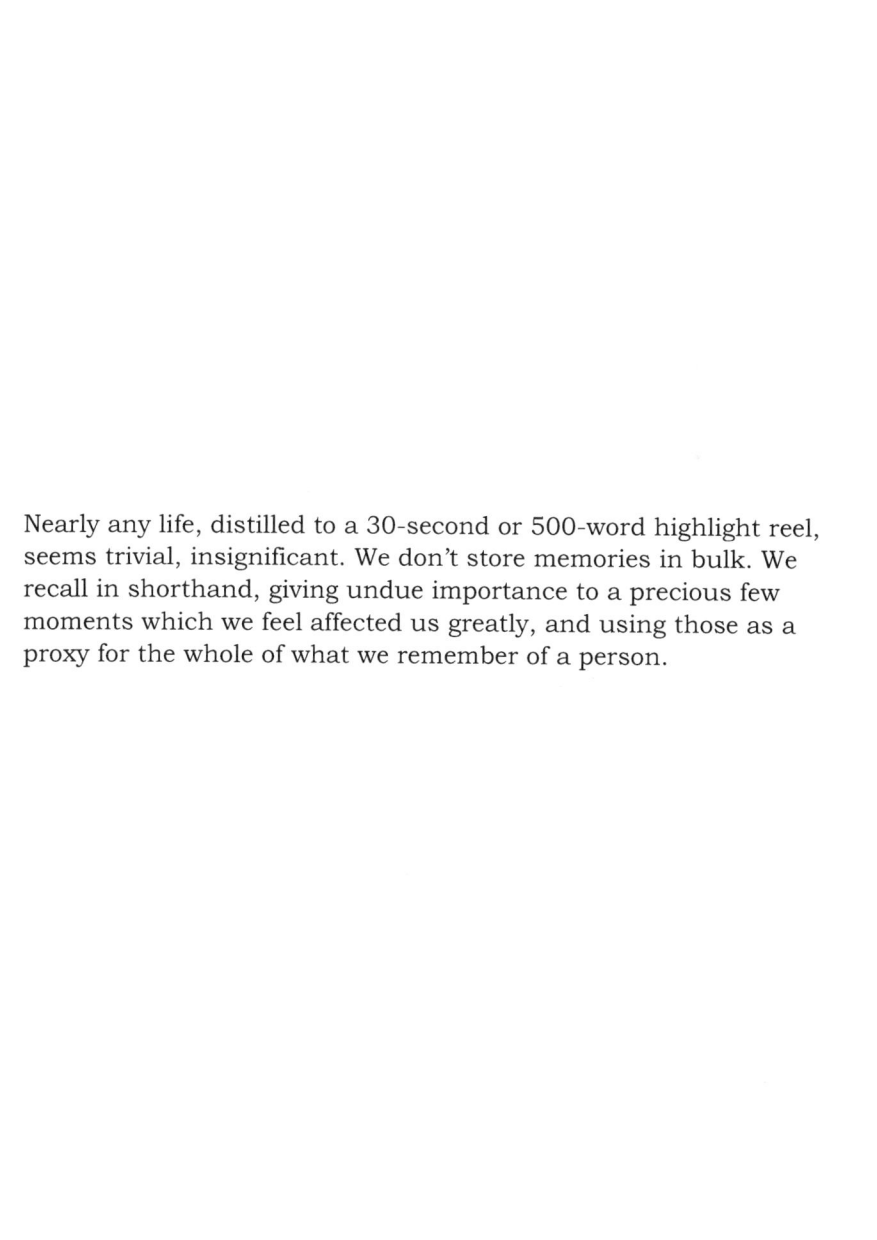

Nearly any life, distilled to a 30-second or 500-word highlight reel, seems trivial, insignificant. We don't store memories in bulk. We recall in shorthand, giving undue importance to a precious few moments which we feel affected us greatly, and using those as a proxy for the whole of what we remember of a person.

Also, I do not tell my roommate for the better part of the day. He is not home when I return from class, so I sit in my room, door closed, crying sobs of varying volume and profundity.

Our apartment is small, and sometimes we do not talk when we are both in it. Later, I pass through the living room, where he is sitting at the table, on my way to the kitchen. "Tom Petty is dead," he says, not looking up from his computer.

"So is my father," I want to, but don't, answer.

I make tea, and bring it out, sitting opposite him at the table. "I'm not, really, handling this well," I begin, and then I tell him.

As we talk, I trace the small letters on the Dell logo of my closed laptop, as if the repetition of my fingers running over the beveled contours will somehow make it hurt less.

Also, I do not post anything on Facebook. For what purpose would that serve?

Posting tragedy porn on social media is not only unwanted and misguided; it belies a very clear psychological shortcoming on behalf of the poster. It shows that you don't delineate between levels of intimacy, between close friends who've known you for the majority of your life and a guy you met once while backpacking in Morocco 6 years ago.

Unless you actively and assiduously monitor your privacy settings, which no one does, you are saying that this moment, this intense, horrible, private moment, deserves equally to be shared with everyone in your "fan base". That this moment deserves to be commemorated with Sad Face emojis and GIFs.

The most significant deaths Facebook should be used to announce or commemorate are those of a pet or an ailing grandparent, which should both occasion the same low-grade amount of grief.

As a result of this decision, though, I am realizing that eventually, I will have to tell everyone I want to know this information individually.

You've always known he'd be gone before you were.

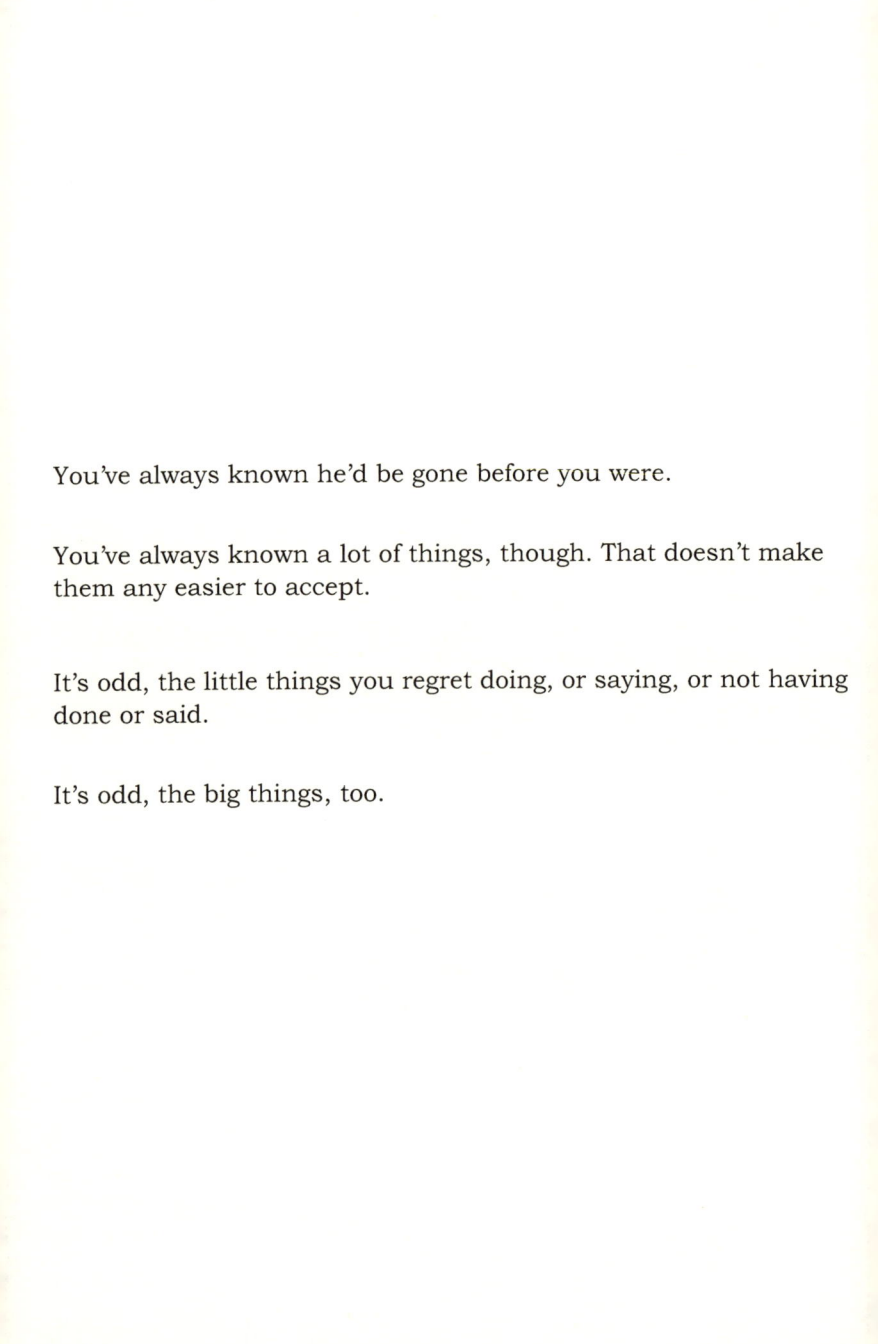

You've always known a lot of things, though. That doesn't make them any easier to accept.

It's odd, the little things you regret doing, or saying, or not having done or said.

It's odd, the big things, too.

Posterity will also show that I taught a 3-hour class at my other campus the day after he died, too. Again, a brief period of normal before heading out to New Jersey to face the situation. Again, the students in front of me don't know what has happened. Again, muscle memory gets me through the morning.

It is amazing the feats we can accomplish when we repress our feelings entirely.

Then a bus to Rockaway Mall, where his wife, his brother, and his brother's wife are waiting to pick me up. A bus I have taken dozens of times, but always with him there waiting for me at ride's end.

The embraces are awkward but sincere. "So what brings you up to New Jersey?" I ask my uncle.

Perhaps it is too soon for that sort of banter.

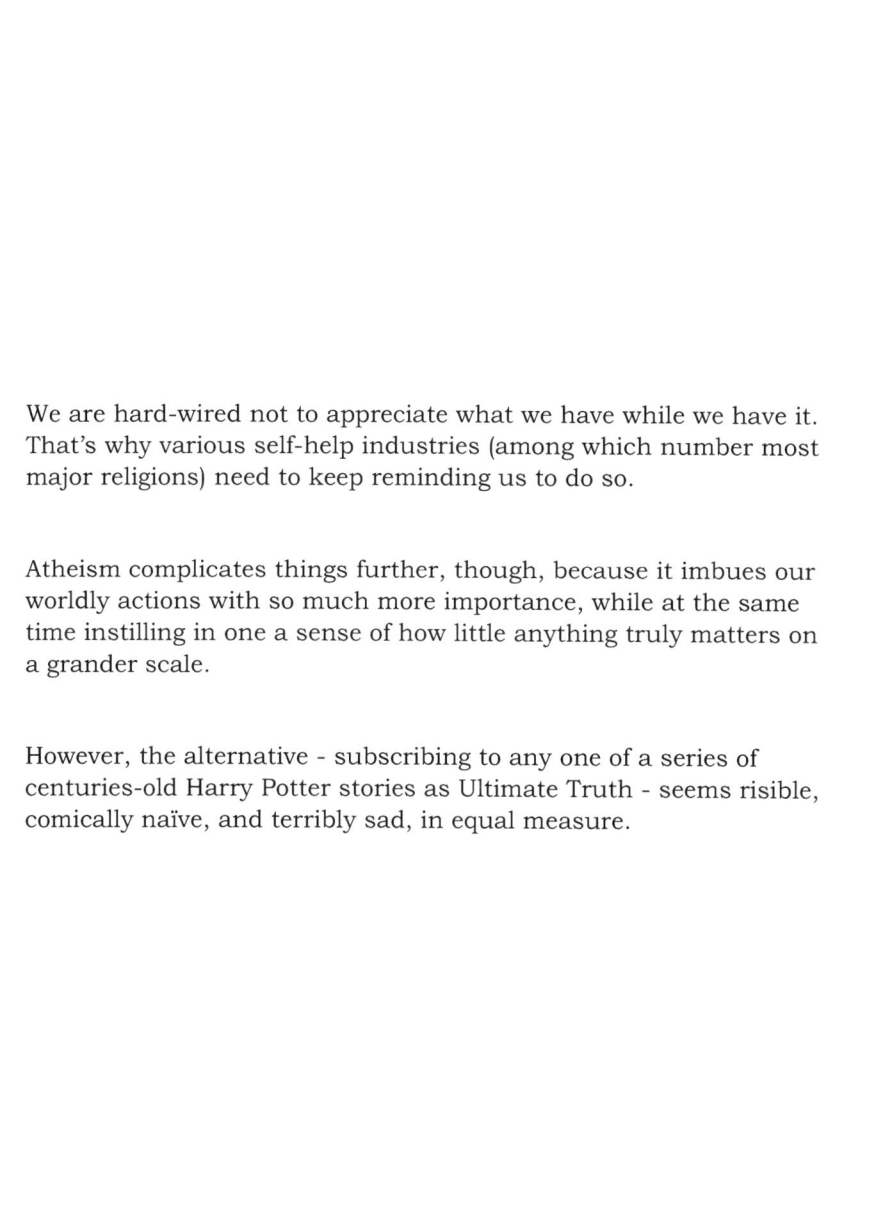

We are hard-wired not to appreciate what we have while we have it. That's why various self-help industries (among which number most major religions) need to keep reminding us to do so.

Atheism complicates things further, though, because it imbues our worldly actions with so much more importance, while at the same time instilling in one a sense of how little anything truly matters on a grander scale.

However, the alternative - subscribing to any one of a series of centuries-old Harry Potter stories as Ultimate Truth - seems risible, comically naïve, and terribly sad, in equal measure.

His chair sits empty as we watch the Yankees win their Wild Card game. I cry uncontrollably when Aaron Judge hits a home run and, for the first time in his young career, lets his emotions show as he is rounding the bases. One of the last times we talked on the phone, on the eve of these playoffs, my father told me, "Their future is so bright." It seems unfair that he will not be here to see any of it.

Also, I've bought playoff tickets for us, 100-level seats to Game 4 of the next round, contingent on them winning the game I have just watched them win. The last time I saw him, at lunch a week (or is it 10 years?) ago, in justifying the high price I'd paid for them, I said to him, "One or both of us may not be here the next time they make it to the playoffs."

If you say enough things, some of them are bound to seem prescient.

"*You* might not be here," he'd responded dismissively, over a plate of hand-pulled noodles, "But *I* will."

Our going to the game was contingent, also, on both of us being alive. Some parameters seem unnecessary to set out, though.

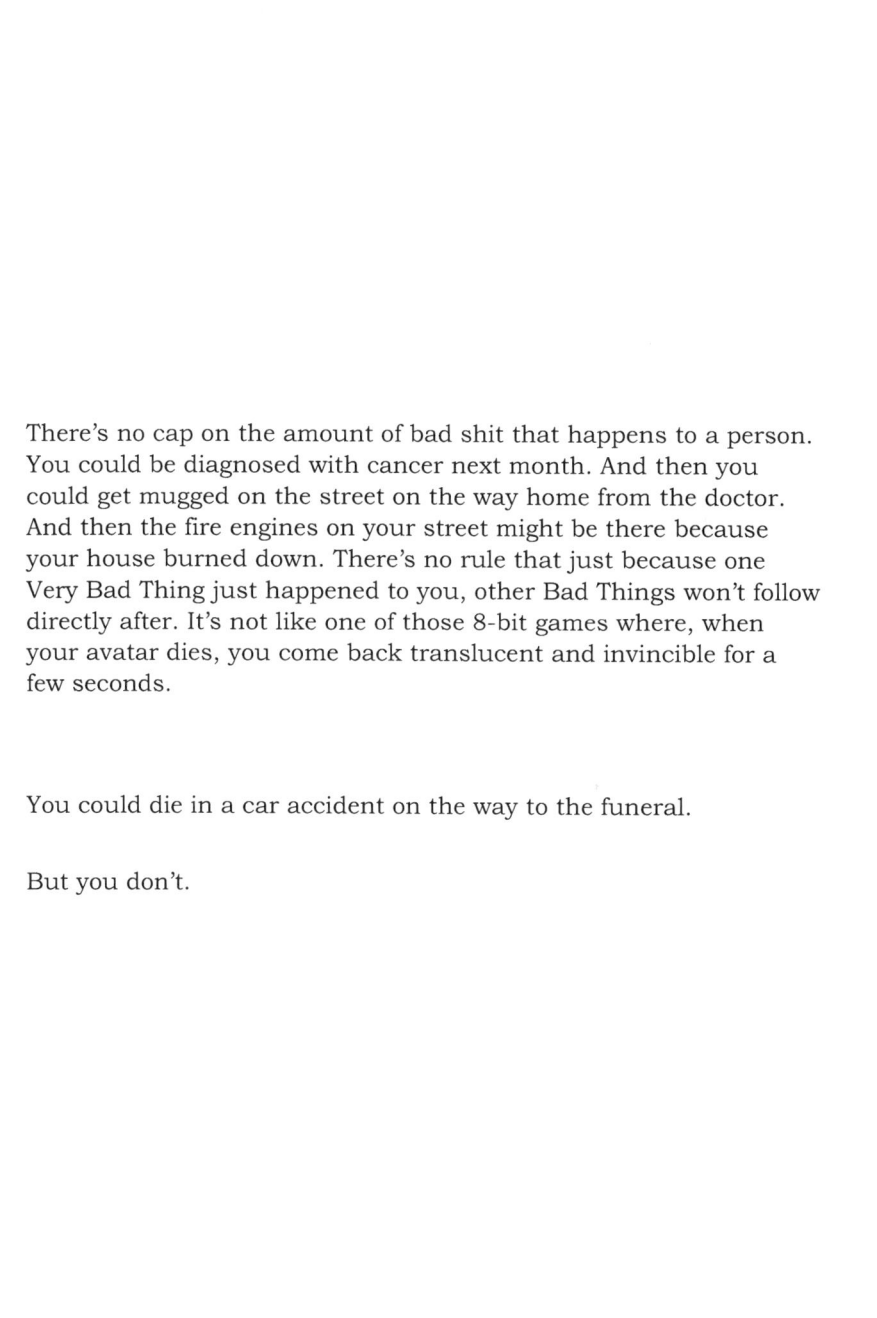

There's no cap on the amount of bad shit that happens to a person. You could be diagnosed with cancer next month. And then you could get mugged on the street on the way home from the doctor. And then the fire engines on your street might be there because your house burned down. There's no rule that just because one Very Bad Thing just happened to you, other Bad Things won't follow directly after. It's not like one of those 8-bit games where, when your avatar dies, you come back translucent and invincible for a few seconds.

You could die in a car accident on the way to the funeral.

But you don't.

Posterity will note that I made two decent jokes in my eulogy of him. That I got through my 5-minute talk without breaking down. My hands were numb enough that it would have been hard to make a fist. But fortunately, I had no need to do so.

Several of the assembled friends and family express appreciation of my words afterwards. Perhaps they are just being polite. There are many people in attendance who I haven't seen in so long that they have actually progressed an entire generation closer to death themselves. There are people now close to his age who were likely closer to my present age the last time I saw them. Many people make vague overtures about meeting up at some point in an indefinite future that both parties know will never materialize.

But "See you at the next funeral", while factually correct, would seem unduly cold.

It is almost certain that, in the entire history of humanity, the list of attendees at two different funerals has never been exactly the same.

The children of his wife's daughter (I have never seriously approached making the psycho-linguistic leap towards referring to them as my "step-nephews") cry a lot at his funeral.

As his wife's first husband has long been out of the picture, I realize later that night that my father was their maternal grandfather.

They called him "Opa", for fuck's sake.

What else about him did I not know? What else about him did I choose to ignore?

And how else might my opinions of him be different had I known some of the things I did not know?

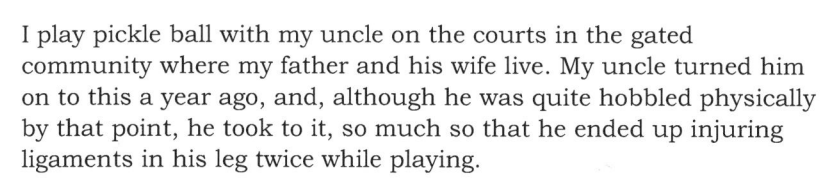

I play pickle ball with my uncle on the courts in the gated community where my father and his wife live. My uncle turned him on to this a year ago, and, although he was quite hobbled physically by that point, he took to it, so much so that he ended up injuring ligaments in his leg twice while playing.

We hit the ball around for about an hour on an unseasonably warm October day. I win a few games, and so does he.

This might have been a fun activity to do with my father. We could have played doubles.

There are a lot of things we could have done.

"*If only I had...*" begins so many thoughts in these moments, none of which ends well.

It's daunting, too, to realize that even as you lament not having shared more with him, you must, if you are honest with yourself, admit the fact that, if he were still here, you probably wouldn't do so anyway.

If he were here now, well, *what*? If he were here now for 15 minutes, or half an hour, you might let spill a stream-of-consciousness confessional that would, at least in the moment, attempt to assuage your guilt - pure, unfiltered, catharsis.

But if he were here for a week? A month? You'd soon find yourself delaying your responses to his text messages again, and digging up excuses not to go and visit him.

We are hard-wired not to appreciate what we have while we have it.

My uncle and his wife pack up to head back down to North Carolina. In the 96 hours that they've been here, I've shared more with them than I had in the 10 years previous. I've spoken more to my father's wife this week than I probably have in the 20 years that I've known her.

It's remarkable what it takes to make most people open up. And by "most people" here, I'm certainly including myself. I have no one else to blame. I'm the one who left the country for the better part of two decades, and didn't make much effort to stay in touch even during the brief times that I have been in the US over that span. I'm the one who didn't answer emails.

The only way I can fairly point a finger here is if I'm looking into a mirror.

From his bathroom, I take a package of disposable razors, a box of earplugs. From his bedroom, I take an unused Yankees beanie with the tag still on it. I take a set of Russian nesting dolls I bought for him in Poland a decade ago. The dolls are painted as famous Yankees throughout time, in uniform. Yogi Berra and Don Mattingly look like twins. I'm not sure who Babe Ruth and Mickey Mantle look like, but it is not Babe Ruth and Mickey Mantle.

The saddest little pirate, claiming the most pathetic of booty.

The next day, my roommate comes to my father's house to pick me up and drive me back to our apartment in the city. "How are you guys?" he asks upon entering the condo.

"Fine, I'm just helping her set up her Tinder account," I tell him. "It's been 5 days, it's time to move on," I say.

She laughs. I laugh. He doesn't.

"A *lady* generally waits at least a week, I've always heard," I continue.

Back at my apartment, I write a letter to a friend from high school I haven't heard from in over 20 years because he happens to be the creator of a popular network television drama that I and my father both watched. I want to thank him, because my father couldn't follow narratives so well, but he stuck with this one. I want to tell him that he and the show were pretty much the last thing I and my father talked about, on the phone, on what would be the last afternoon of his life.

I also find on my hard drive, revise, and send a letter I wrote to a girl I met in New York in one of my teacher training seminars 9 years ago, a student who I had a crush on. I never sent the letter to her then, because at the time I was in love with a person I thought I'd be with for the rest of my life (a relationship which ended 6 months later). She is now in Brazil, and I have chatted with her on occasion on Facebook. She doesn't post much. Almost impossible to stalk.

Both people respond, my friend to say thank you, and that he will pass my letter on to the cast and writers of the show. The girl to say thank you, and that yes, in 2008, she did have a crush on me, too. But now she is married, though she appreciates the sentiment nonetheless, and sends her condolences.

In general, it is too much to ask for Hollywood endings.

Death is a part of life like the credits are a part of the movie. Very few people stick around to watch, and the ones who do generally only do so because they have an overly vested interest in seeing a name they recognize in there somewhere.

And "closure" only exists for the person who ceases existing.

A week or so After, my roommate, a friend from college, asks if I'd like him to bring a joke sign from our freshman year he still has stored in his mother's house to hang in our apartment. "*No Parents Allowed*", it says.

"Maybe I should get one that says, '*No Parents Alive*'", I respond.

"Oh," he says. "Well, now."

What is "too soon"?

And isn't its opposite even worse?

The day after I return to the city, I go to renew my monthly Metrocard at one of the kiosks in the station, and after I insert my debit card and type my PIN, the screen cycles for two or three minutes before saying that the transaction cannot be processed. I try again at the machine next to it, with the same result. The MTA worker in the station booth says the system is "acting up" today, and lets me through the gate without paying.

Later on, I buy a monthly pass at another station downtown. When I look at my bank account online later that night, I have been charged $121 twice. This has never happened before.

There's no cap on the Bad Shit that can happen to you over a given period of time.

I'll never have to worry about what to get him for his birthday or for Christmas again. This realization makes me cry upon its formulation.

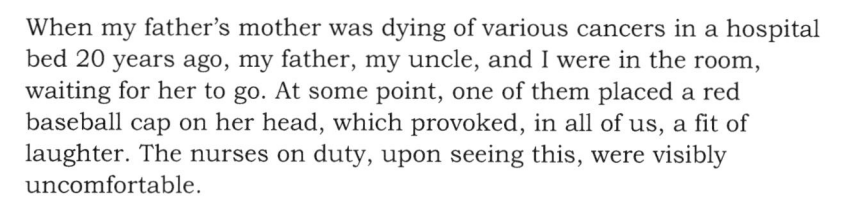

When my father's mother was dying of various cancers in a hospital bed 20 years ago, my father, my uncle, and I were in the room, waiting for her to go. At some point, one of them placed a red baseball cap on her head, which provoked, in all of us, a fit of laughter. The nurses on duty, upon seeing this, were visibly uncomfortable.

But who makes the rules here, with Death? And who's ignorant enough to think that you have to follow them?

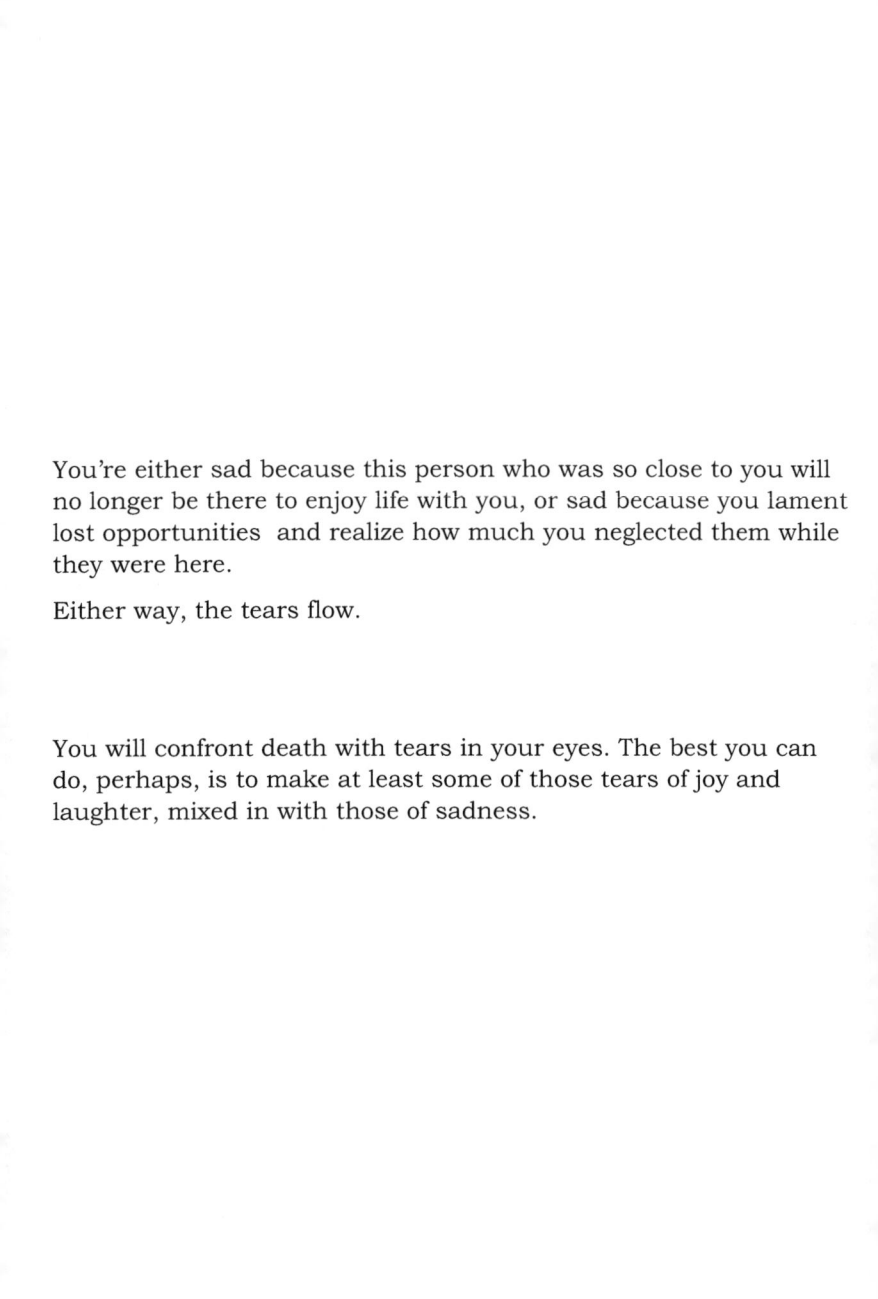

You're either sad because this person who was so close to you will no longer be there to enjoy life with you, or sad because you lament lost opportunities and realize how much you neglected them while they were here.

Either way, the tears flow.

You will confront death with tears in your eyes. The best you can do, perhaps, is to make at least some of those tears of joy and laughter, mixed in with those of sadness.

This is a book about Death.

About, in both senses of the preposition.

    about: *with respect to, considering the theme of*

But also,

    about: *in proximity to, in the area of*

As in, "A man about town".

It's odd, the things you regret.

When I was 16, and still being forced to go to therapy in the wake of my mother's death, I remember I was prescribed Prozac. This was pre-Internet, and even if Google had existed, there wouldn't have been much information on the drug, because it had just been released.

I did not want to take it. I did not want a chemical altering who I was (odd to consider this now, after the 20+ years of often prolific non-prescription drug use that followed).

My father did not give me the option to refuse. So I would take the pills, leave the room he was in, and then spit them out into the toilet.

At some point, he found out about this. I don't remember how, but it didn't take long. There followed, then, a physical tussle, in our kitchen one afternoon, he physically trying to force a pill down my throat, I wriggling away like a recalcitrant dog refusing its tapeworm medication.

The fight did not last long; the only scars were emotional.

At some point, later on, I know that we talked about this. I know that he said he felt bad, and I know that he understood why I acted the way I had.

Still, though, he was only looking out for me.

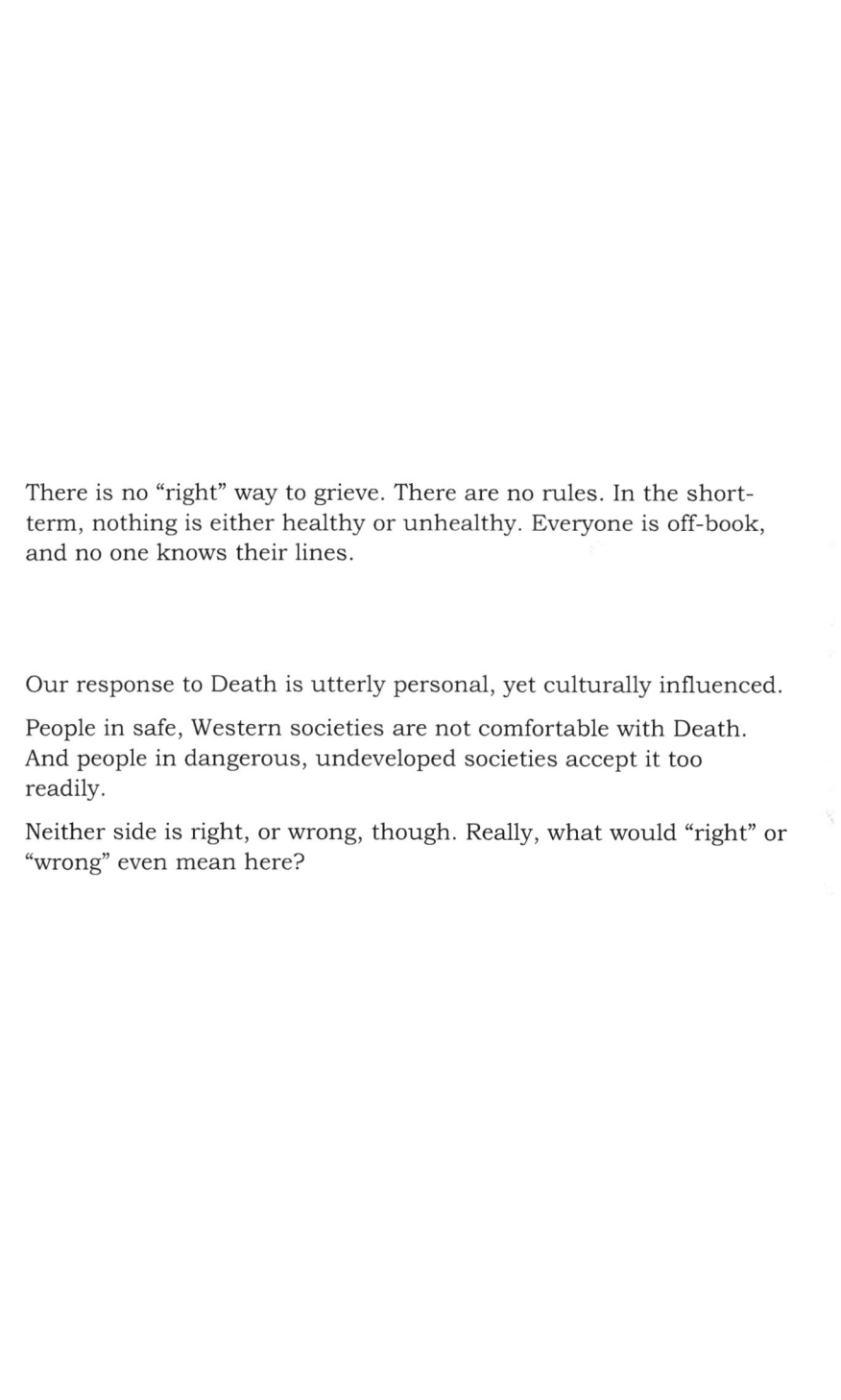

There is no "right" way to grieve. There are no rules. In the short-term, nothing is either healthy or unhealthy. Everyone is off-book, and no one knows their lines.

Our response to Death is utterly personal, yet culturally influenced.

People in safe, Western societies are not comfortable with Death. And people in dangerous, undeveloped societies accept it too readily.

Neither side is right, or wrong, though. Really, what would "right" or "wrong" even mean here?

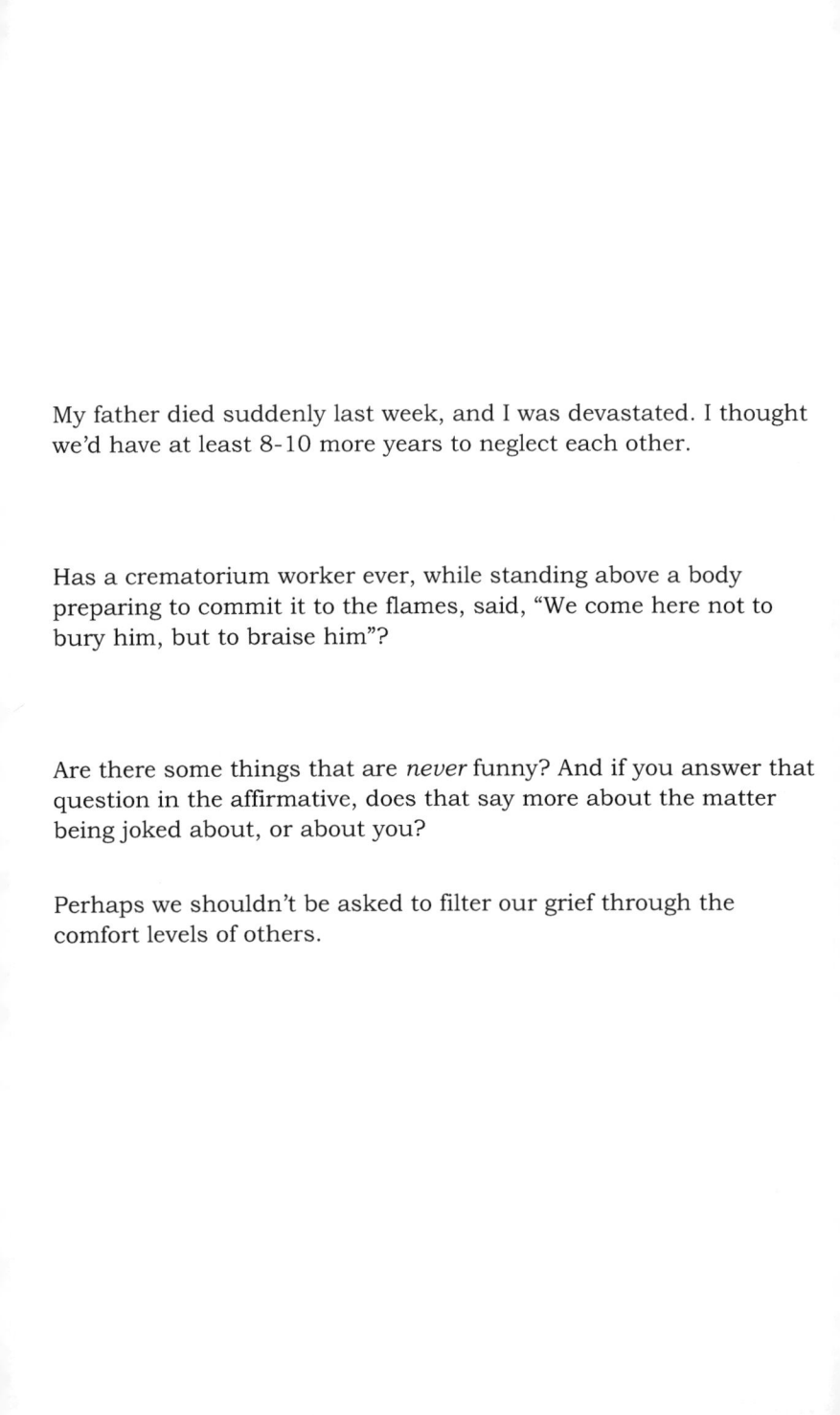

My father died suddenly last week, and I was devastated. I thought we'd have at least 8-10 more years to neglect each other.

Has a crematorium worker ever, while standing above a body preparing to commit it to the flames, said, "We come here not to bury him, but to braise him"?

Are there some things that are *never* funny? And if you answer that question in the affirmative, does that say more about the matter being joked about, or about you?

Perhaps we shouldn't be asked to filter our grief through the comfort levels of others.

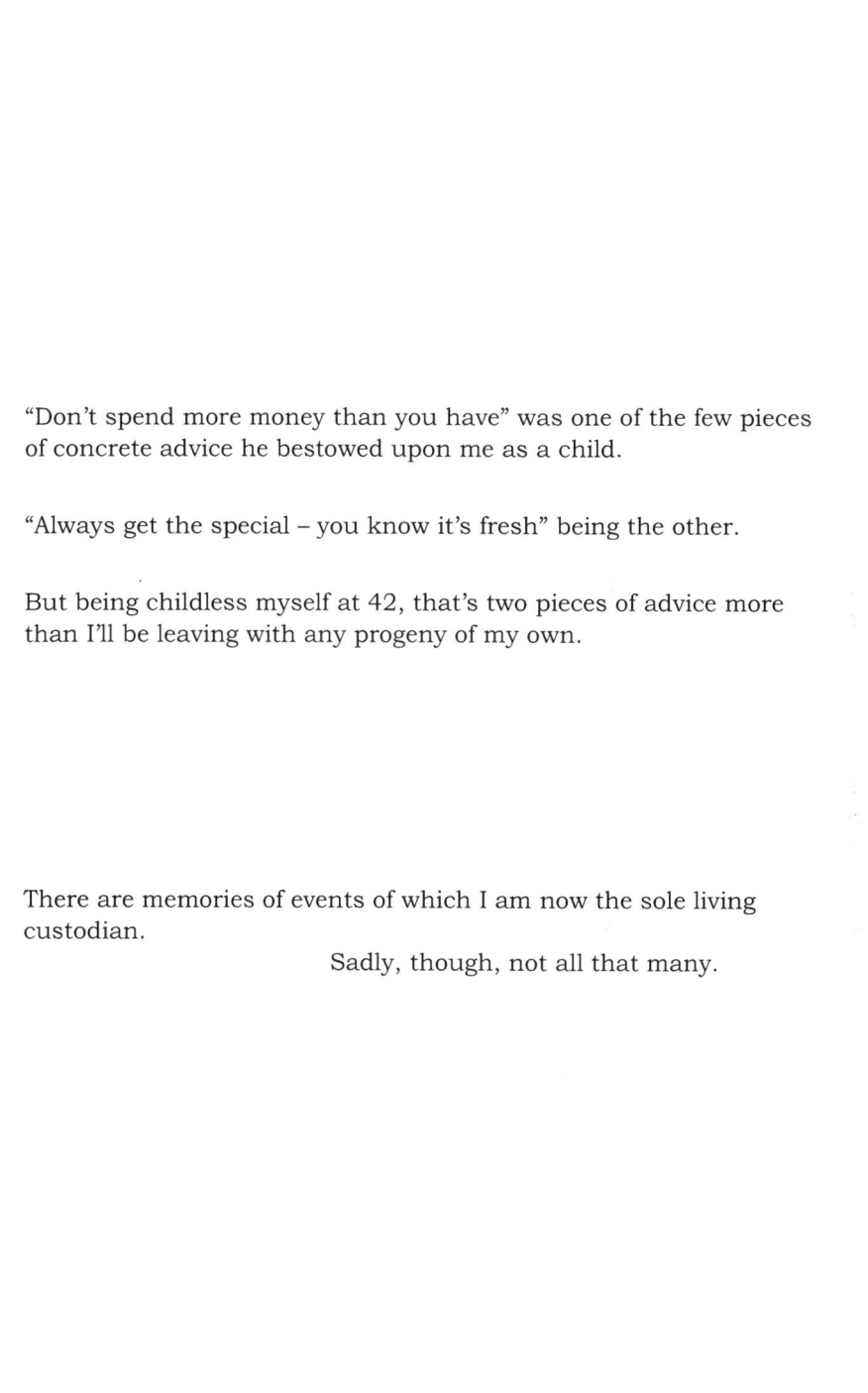

"Don't spend more money than you have" was one of the few pieces of concrete advice he bestowed upon me as a child.

"Always get the special – you know it's fresh" being the other.

But being childless myself at 42, that's two pieces of advice more than I'll be leaving with any progeny of my own.

There are memories of events of which I am now the sole living custodian.
                    Sadly, though, not all that many.

At some point early on, I was told by my parents that my first word, my first attempt to name and classify, was not some form of "*ma*" or "*pa*", but rather, my pointing to a record, and saying "*ook*".

For a long time, I took this to have been an amusing portent of my desires, in my early to mid-twenties, to be a DJ.

Only later did it come to me, of an afternoon's introspection, that 70's LPs were often doubles, and so opened in the middle, and really, what I had chosen to denominate with my first intelligible speech act, was, however mistaken the object, a book.

Which now serves to explain conveniently why most days, I am happiest sitting at home in a comfortable chair with a warm mug of tea, lost in the printed word.

But I'm the only one who knows that now.

He said to me on more than one occasion, with apparent sincerity, that the "best" job he'd ever had, in terms of what made him happy, was when he was bagging groceries in high school at the Shop Rite in Rochelle Park, New Jersey. He liked working out the geometry of the boxes and cans, I guess. He said he was quite good at it.

As an adult, he worked as a salesperson for a bottling company right out of college for a bit. And then he sold plastic bags. For 40 years. That was all he did. He worked for different companies in different states, but he never left the industry.

I used to joke (though not to him) that this was just about the least interesting field one could conceive of. As a young adult, meeting people, getting to know them, it was literally a conversation-stopper:

"What does your dad do?"

"He sells plastic bags."

"..."

What's the follow-up there? "Are they big?" "What color?"

Some sons get roped into the family industry. Others want in. For me, I was never sure what I wanted to be (not sure I am now). I only knew what I *didn't* want – to sell plastic bags.

But plastic bags paid for a lot of Nintendo cartridges. Plastic bags put me through college without a student loan. Plastic bags paid for a lot of international flights in my 20s. Plastic bags made it possible for me not to incur any real debt despite my not earning a real salary until I was 31 years old.

So maybe I shouldn't be such a fucking ingrate. Maybe I should offer up a little respect here. Even if it's posthumous.

Most people are not special. Statistically speaking, the chances that you will, over the course of an average lifetime, take any action which will adversely affect a large group of people (for bad or for good) is almost infinitesimally small.

Still, it feels like most lives could be better spent.

Everyone feels that they are a bit better than average. Though if you don't think you are, it's very hard to do anything at all.

In most measures in life, most of us will perform somewhere close to the mean. That's what an "average" is.

Yet who wants to spend time with someone who is, by their own admission, "average"?

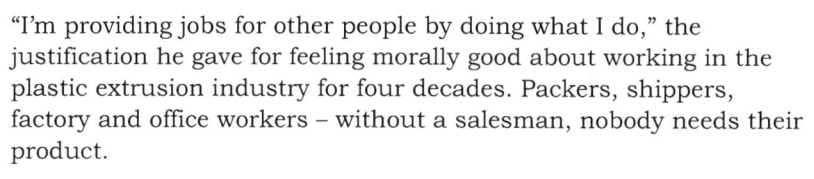

"I'm providing jobs for other people by doing what I do," the justification he gave for feeling morally good about working in the plastic extrusion industry for four decades. Packers, shippers, factory and office workers – without a salesman, nobody needs their product.

To his credit, he rarely waxed philosophical.

Yet still he managed to beget one neurotic, existential toxic waste dump of a person as his sole progeny.

The apple may not fall far from the tree, but sometimes the landing does bruise it somewhat.

Did I have an "average" relationship with my father?

I know people who are far closer to their parents than I was to my father, sometimes to a point which actually seems unhealthy. I also know people who don't have any relationship with their (still-living) parents at all, for reasons ranging from somewhat valid to farcically insignificant.

If I were to assign to the former group the value of "1", and to the latter, a "10", I'd say my father and I were somewhere around a 6.5. Not great, but nowhere near a standard deviation away from the norm.

It could have been better.

But you could say that about pretty much anything.

Still, I can't really remember a genuinely good time he and I had together in the past 20 years. At least nothing longer or more substantive than a meal or the shared viewing of an entertaining TV program.

And perhaps I'm being generous to myself and to his memory by adding "really" there.

He did, though, insist that I keep a $20 bill folded in the inner pocket of my wallet, when I was old enough to be places without him.

"This way, in case there's an emergency, you'll never run out of money."

So I did. And I never have.

So there's that.

I go back to work. It's only been a week, but the alternative, staying home and grieving, seems less attractive and less healthy. The dean, my boss, asked me if she should tell the students what had happened, and I'd responded that she should just say there was "a death in the family", that that would be specific enough. I then got an email from an Iranian girl offering condolences for the loss of my father, so I guess the dean didn't keep it as vague as I'd hoped.

These students know me - in intensive language classes, you are spending 5 hours a day with people. And they aren't just coworkers, sharing an office with you, because the interaction is sustained and engrossing. Being anything close to a "good" teacher means caring about your students. Even though it would be generous to say that we are "friends", for at least some of them, I am the American they know best.

It is odd teaching them now, knowing that they know. I know how it feels to want to say something serious in a language you aren't entirely comfortable with - often, you end up just avoiding the topic, for fear of sounding like a 5-year old. At some point, near the end of the day, I see that they are not-so-surreptitiously passing around a card to sign, and I know what it is, and this makes it difficult for me to concentrate. As the day ends, and I dismiss them, a young kid, a friendly, angelic Colombian whose parents sent him to the US when he came out to them because they thought somehow being here might "work the gay out of him" gives me the card and shares the group's condolences. I nod, and the words don't come out, though the tears start to.

In 18 years as a teacher, I have never cried in front of a class. I sit down facing the computer in the corner of the room, so as not to have to look at them, but two girls, Iranians, friends who came to the US together, do not leave. One of them, the more confident speaker of the two, tells me that they are sorry, that they know it is hard, that they wish they could express more eloquently what they want to say at this moment, and she hugs me. And now I cannot say that I have never cried in front of a class anymore.

I bring my roommate to the Yankees' game that I'd intended to take my father to. The seats are great. It is an uncomfortably muggy mid-October evening. It does not feel as bad as I'd imagined it would. It does not feel like much of anything at all.

My father would have complained about the heat. It is so unseasonably hot that he might not have come at all. "Take Keith," he would have said.

So I imagine that's what he said, and I imagine that's what I did.

The Yankees win. The Yankees win.

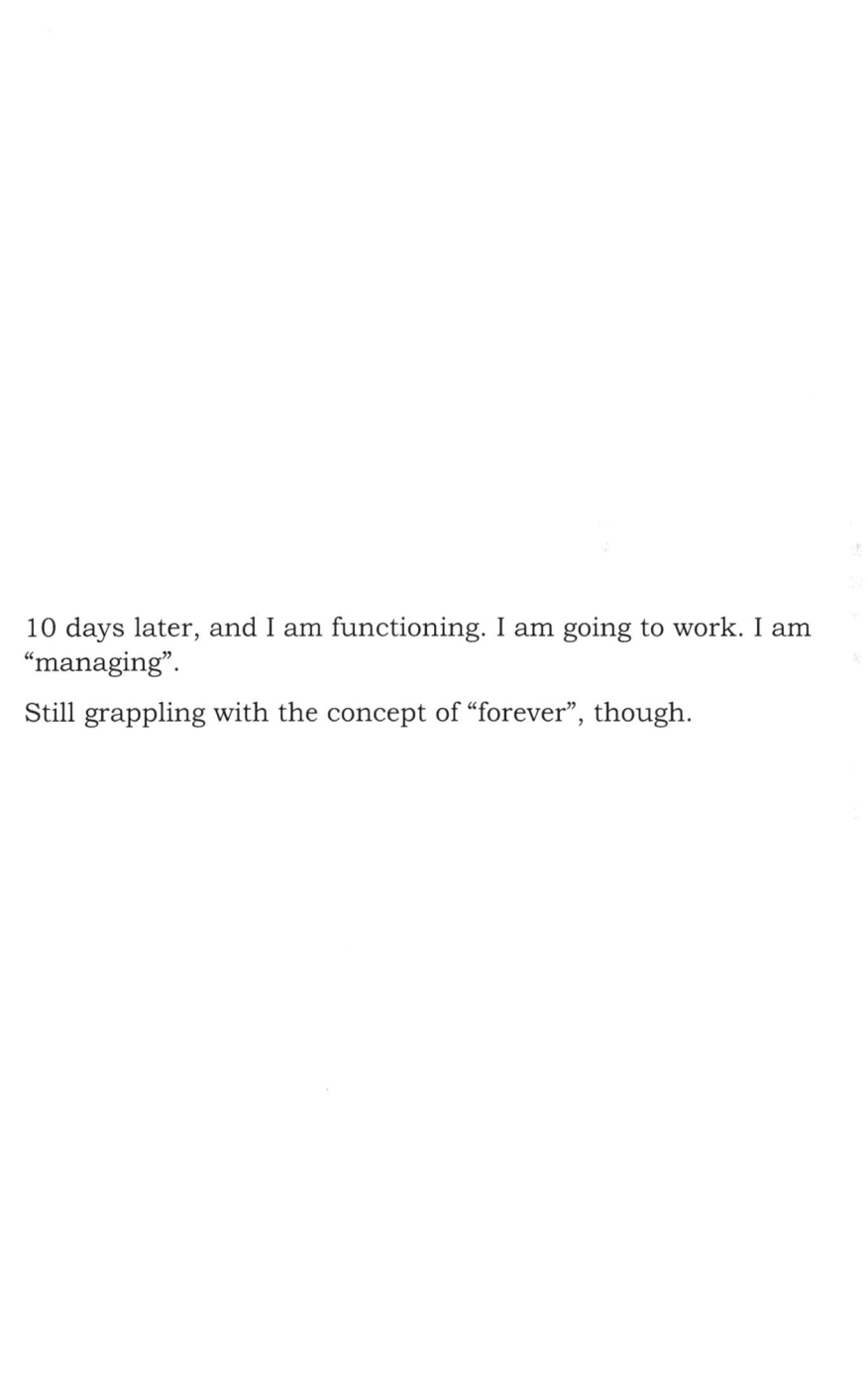

10 days later, and I am functioning. I am going to work. I am "managing".

Still grappling with the concept of "forever", though.

I do not get drunk or high in the aftermath. For 10 days, I go to sleep at something close to a normal hour, but wake up as though having been shocked with a Taser at 4AM. It is dark, and I am alone. There is no one to talk to, and I don't know what I would want to say even if there were.

It is very difficult to know what to do.

No one has a copy of the script here, and no one has memorized their lines.

Also, I am dizzy most of the time. Like, so dizzy I almost might fall down.

So there's that.

He had been complaining of dizziness the last few times I saw him.

Is my vertigo iatrogenic? Like the random chest pains I've been having?

A sympathetic infarction.

But, how good did you *expect* to feel at this point?

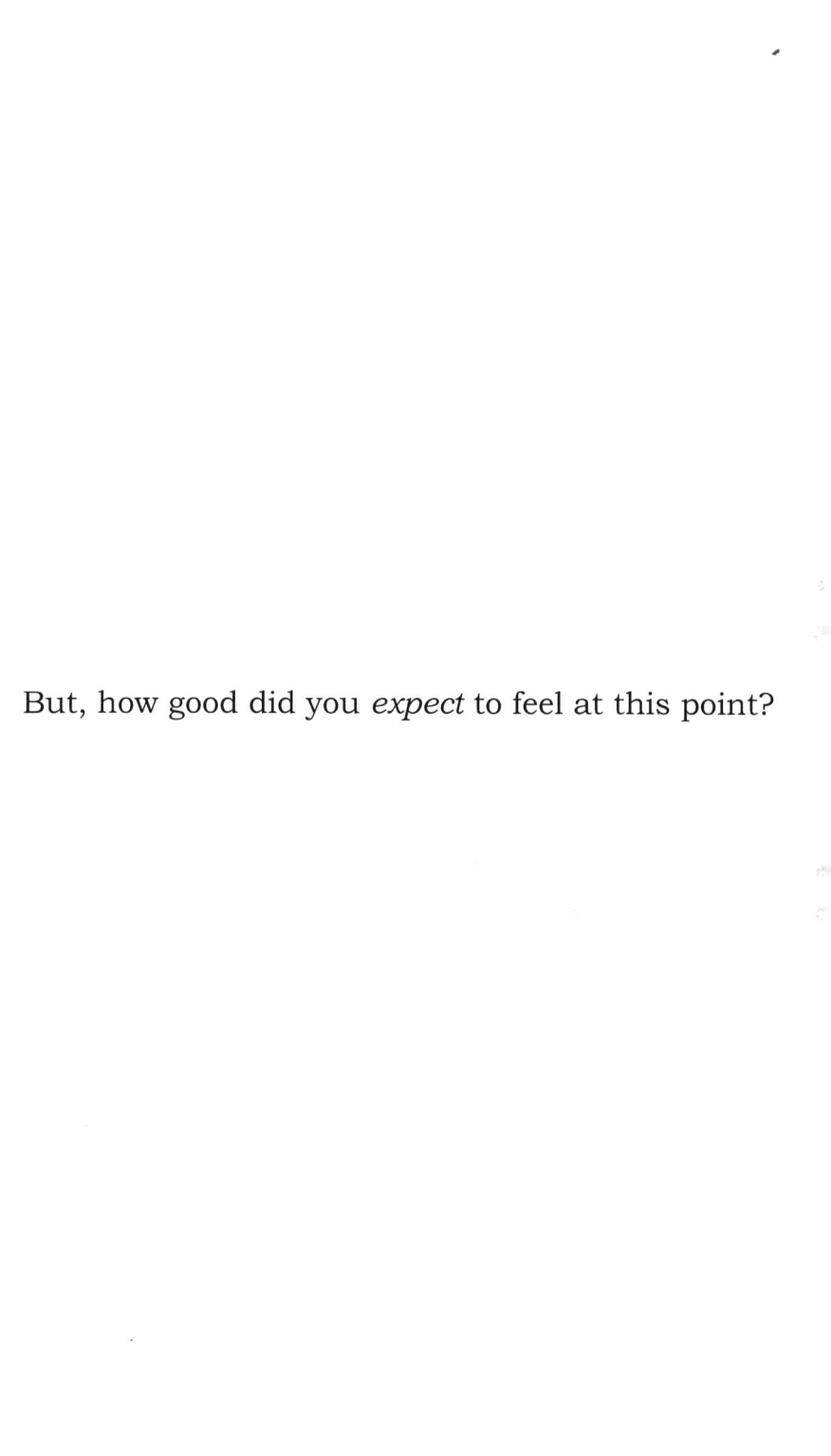

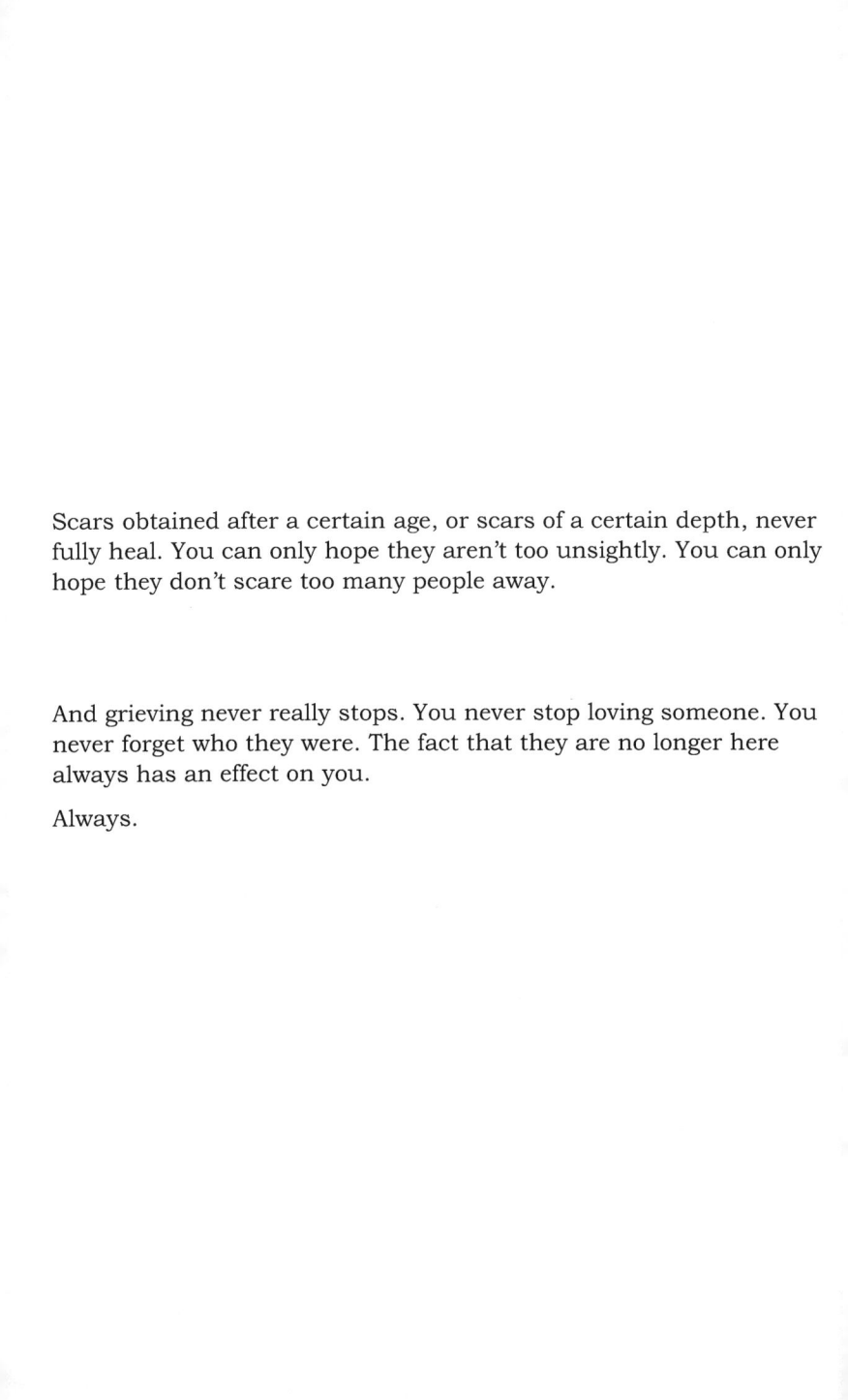

Scars obtained after a certain age, or scars of a certain depth, never fully heal. You can only hope they aren't too unsightly. You can only hope they don't scare too many people away.

And grieving never really stops. You never stop loving someone. You never forget who they were. The fact that they are no longer here always has an effect on you.

Always.

The last communication I received from him, an SMS saying "Larry David is on!"

"We need him now more than ever," my response, his a thumbs up.

He died watching the season premiere of *Curb Your Enthusiasm*, the show's return from a 6-year hiatus.

It was a good episode.

But also, this. My maternal grandmother died a year ago, at 95, after spending nearly 4 years in a semi-conscious, speechless, completely bedridden state. On many occasions, my father said to me, "If I get like that, just pull the plug. Just put a pillow over my head."

So, could it not be argued, then, that his death was the best of all possible deaths?

A sudden pain, a clutch at the chest, and then a release.

He died in his favorite chair. In front of his wide flat screen TV. After kissing his wife goodnight.

No mess. No tears. No hospice.

No waiting. No prolonging the inevitable.

Effectively, it was a fatal one-car crash on a deserted road, all in the comfort of his own home.

Music still hurts. Pretty much all of it.

Podcasts seem safer at the moment. It's good to hear people talk about something that doesn't matter.

I will never have to take care of a parent as they slip into senescence and invalidity. My mother was dead before I began the 8th grade, and my father, now gone, too, still some years before needing a caregiver. I will never have to dress or wash or clean the two people who provided such services to me until I was old enough to do so for myself. I feel, somehow, like I've dodged a bullet, avoiding this sad, filial inconvenience. Or, conversely, yet again, I will have found a very concrete way to never truly have to grow up.

I go to a second Yankees playoff game, this time alone. This is the ALCS. I bring the beanie I found in his room in the days After. Two nights ago, it was colder, and I put it on in the apartment as I was watching the game. They won. Last night, as I was walking uptown after teaching a private class, I put it on as I bounced from bar window to bar window, catching bits of the game here and there and embracing what it means to be in New York at this time of year. They won again.

Tonight, it is warmer again. I keep the beanie in the bag I carried into the stadium. The crowd is raucous and vulgar. The Yankees win again, easily. I give reluctant, ill-timed high fives to the people seated around me because to refuse to do so would be as well-received as kneeling during the national anthem. The stadium is completely full, but the seat next to me remains empty throughout the game.

Coincidence?

Yes, that's literally all it is. I bought a single seat online. This was probably the pair to that seat, which no one else wanted to purchase only to attend alone.

On the big screen above center field, late in the game, they show a montage of Reggie Jackson's 3-HR World Series, which happened 40 years ago today. Reggie was his favorite player. I have seen the replays of these home runs so many times it is easy to feel as though I was actually there to witness them.

I don't want to be a solitary, middle-aged man sitting alone at a playoff game that the home team is winning and crying at a video on the Jumbotron. I hold most of it in with Lamaze breaths and clenched teeth.

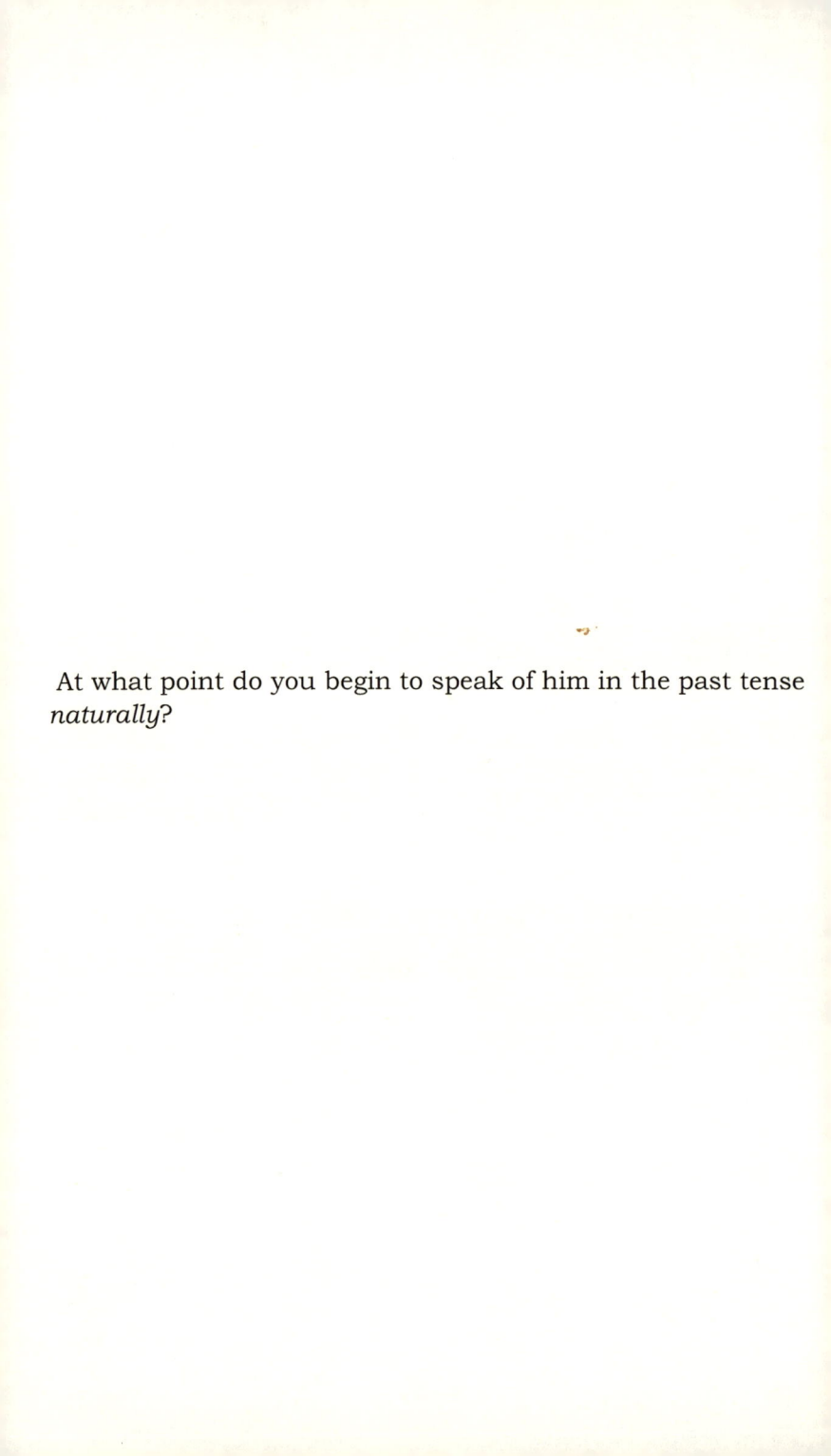

At what point do you begin to speak of him in the past tense *naturally*?

I watch the US Men's Soccer Team get embarrassed by Trinidad and Tobago as they fail to qualify for the World Cup. Watching this team at international events has probably been the closest thing to "fanatical" sports behavior that I have ever displayed. I have woken up at 2AM to watch World Cup games, I have cancelled classes to watch World Cup games, I have rearranged vacations to watch World Cup games. If you had told me two weeks ago that our team would not be heading to a World Cup for the first time since I was 11, I would have been devastated.

Now, though, if I feel anything, it's relief - at least I won't have to watch the draw in December nervously. I won't have to miss classes to watch games next summer.

It's funny, the things we think are important, until something important happens.

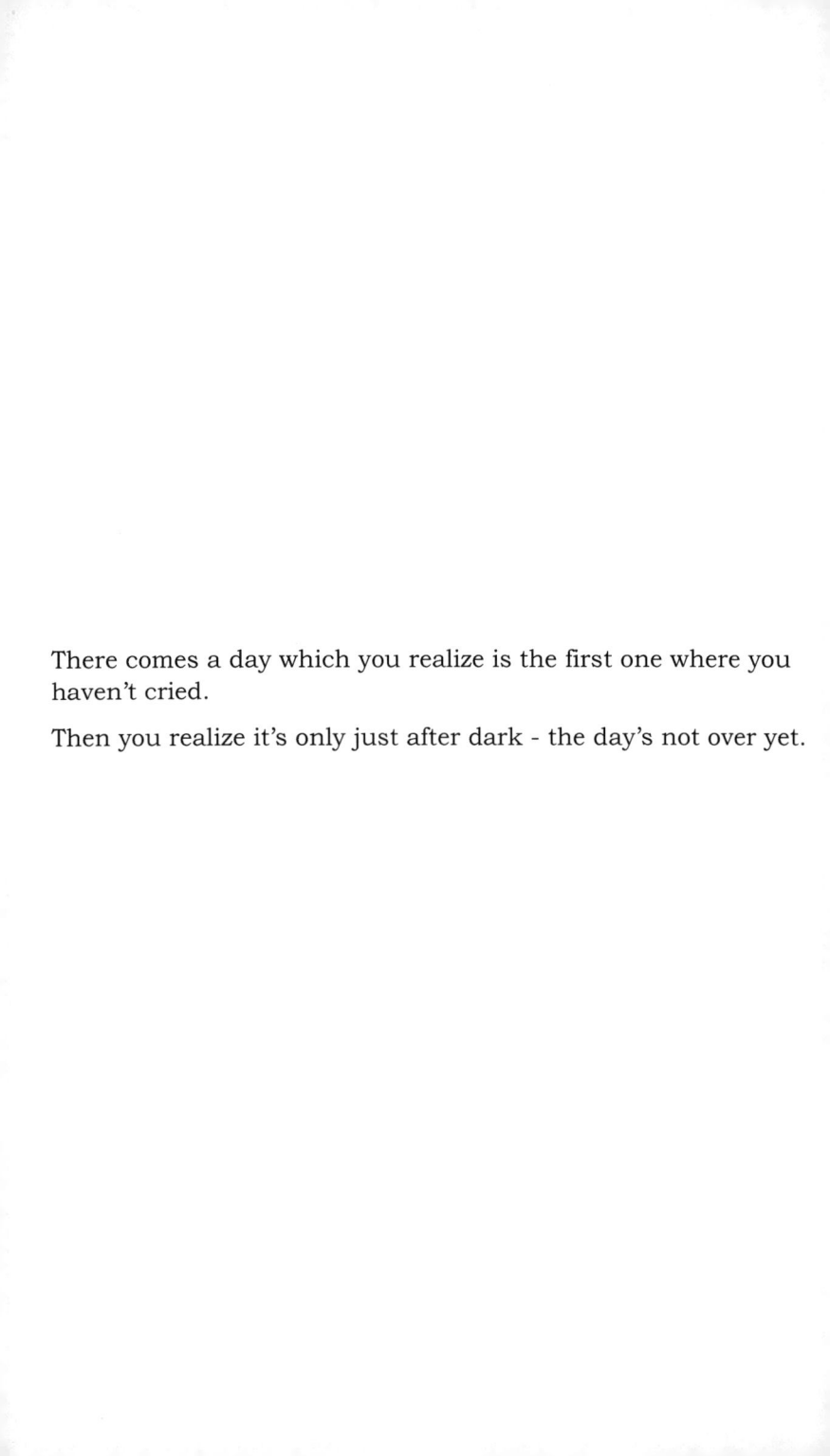

There comes a day which you realize is the first one where you haven't cried.

Then you realize it's only just after dark - the day's not over yet.

I begin to research bereavement groups online. I leave a message with one therapist, who calls back to say that she does not have a group running at the moment. She directs me to a colleague, who has a group starting the same night. "I do want to start soon," I tell him, "but maybe not *right* now." He tells me he will call me back, and then does not. A third group leader tells me he doesn't even permit someone to join a group until the parent has been gone for three months, which seems to me to be an inordinately long amount of time if you are in need of the comfort such a group could provide.

I mean, I'm not going to be sitting around here grieving indefinitely, I feel like telling him. Let's get this shit addressed, overcome, and boxed away with all the other life issues I no longer feel the need or capacity to confront.

I have not been in any type of therapy since the grieving process for my mother was deemed "completed" nearly 25 years ago. On various levels, I am ideologically opposed to therapy and the therapeutic process (imagine a mechanic who told you you needed to bring your car back to him regularly over the course of a year, or a physician who said you needed to see him once a week, indefinitely, for maintenance – you would seek out another service provider pretty damn quickly, I'd assume).

But now, it seems like talking about this, or, at least listening to others talk about this, is something I'd like to do.

Maybe I'm just lonely, and it's a loneliness that didn't start 15 days ago.

At a certain point, all parents want for their children is that they are happy. In this, I fear, I failed him, as for long stretches of time I made little attempt to hide my general ennui and discontent.

I'm sorry, Dad, it's not you – I'm just not that impressed with life.

I said that to him in so many words on various occasions. Though it couldn't have felt good for him to hear it.

It is very easy to overcome someone else's grief. In the aftermath of a death, in the initial cycle of confession and condolence, you will be asked how you are feeling, how you are managing, so many times that you will become dismissive, perhaps even annoyed. You will make recourse to the simple shorthand conventions of the event, that there are "good days and bad days", "ups and downs", as though such ebbs and flows were not present in your life before.

But then, just weeks after, the questions stop, though the grieving does not. There will be a first World Series, a first Christmas, a first birthday (yours and theirs), without the person. Likely, no one will be asking you how you are managing on those days.

It does not even take the advent of anything special to occasion a recurrence of grief. There are articles you would forward to him, restaurants you'd like him to try. Whether or not he would read that article or enjoy that restaurant is irrelevant. The fact that you would want to share them with him but cannot is what matters.

Ups and downs.

There will be "*Remember whens*?" to which no one can answer in the affirmative. There will be inconsequential things in your life that derive importance simply from having someone with a vested interest in All Things You to wax concerned over, and when you realize, in those moments, that that person is no longer there, you will be glad that no one is asking you how you are doing, because they would not be capable of or amenable to contemplating your response.

Eight days before November and it is still balmy in New York City.

"This isn't normal," people will complain. But we are wrong. It is the new normal. We just aren't used to it yet.

In 25 years, when it is 90 degrees Fahrenheit in December, people who are kids now but will be my present age then will say, "When I was in high school, it was only in the 90's until the end of *October*. This isn't *normal*, what's happening now."

As for me, though, I haven't been in the US in October since 2008, so I don't know what is or isn't "normal" here. It feels normal to me not having a father I can see this time of year.

Yes, everything is perfectly normal.

Whatever works, man. Whatever gets you through the day.

I take a train to spend the weekend down at the family beach house at the Jersey Shore. It is the first time I've been down there since I helped an aunt and uncle remove post-Sandy debris on a sunny January afternoon five years ago. I thought, at that point, that my two aunts, the custodians of the place, would just write it off and get rid of it. Instead, they sat on it, and actually got around to fixing it up this past summer.

My aunt picks me up at the nearest train station, and we arrive back at the house shortly after darkness falls. I cry a little when I see the backyard, an Elysian Field of my youth where I used to make my grandfather throw me fly balls to shag until his arm got sore, where I used the patio to play an elaborate solo version of wall ball which pitted imaginary teams against each other in a league or my own invention which convened every summer.

There is barely enough space for a table and set of deck chairs on the patio. You could traverse the back yard in about six long strides. Yet 30 years ago it was a vast expanse of land.

As a child, it takes so little to amuse. Then as an adult, almost nothing does.

The family house used to be the largest on the block and now it's the smallest. You could see it from the corner, you could use it to orient yourself. Now it is dwarfed by Sopranos McMansions, 3-story monstrosities with multiple decks, houses too bloated for the modest plots of land they sit on. Even the place next door, a derelict shanty lived in by an alcoholic couple who left it to an alcoholic son, is now an immaculate split-level home. My aunt tells me the kid had it rebuilt with FEMA money after Sandy.

God Bless America.

On the Boardwalk, the other Valhalla of my childhood, little remains. A hurricane in 2012 teamed up with a fire in 2013 to erase pretty much everything. If not for the inky, quiet ocean next to it, you wouldn't even realize you were in the same place. The arcades no longer have video games. There is a food stand selling açaí bowls. No more funnel cakes. No more big pretzels.

Even if you don't change, everything changes around you.

My father didn't like this place. He didn't like the house, which didn't have central air conditioning, and he didn't like spending time with his sisters-in-law in a cramped space. He didn't like the beach, which was crowded with families and not all that clean. And he certainly didn't like the boardwalk, where I pestered him to give me endless rolls of quarters to quite literally throw away at games of chance and jerky, janky Magic Claws.

It's good to be here again.

Over two successive nights, in a few different bars on the boardwalk, I watch Games 6 and 7 of the ALCS. On the first night, the bouncer asks me for ID, and when I thank him for doing so, he says "I didn't realize you were *THAT* old!" when he looks at it. I chat, a bit, with the townies. Although we were all born in the same state, I feel as though we are not even from the same country.

On the first night, an old guy with his old girl buys everyone around him lemon drop shots for his birthday. I blend in. A little.

As much as I do anywhere.

The Yankees lose both games, and are eliminated from the postseason.

It's generally too much to ask for a Hollywood ending.

On the walk home of the second night, mildly intoxicated, I almost instinctively go to send a text to him to commiserate.

How long until his nonexistence is not something I have lapses about?

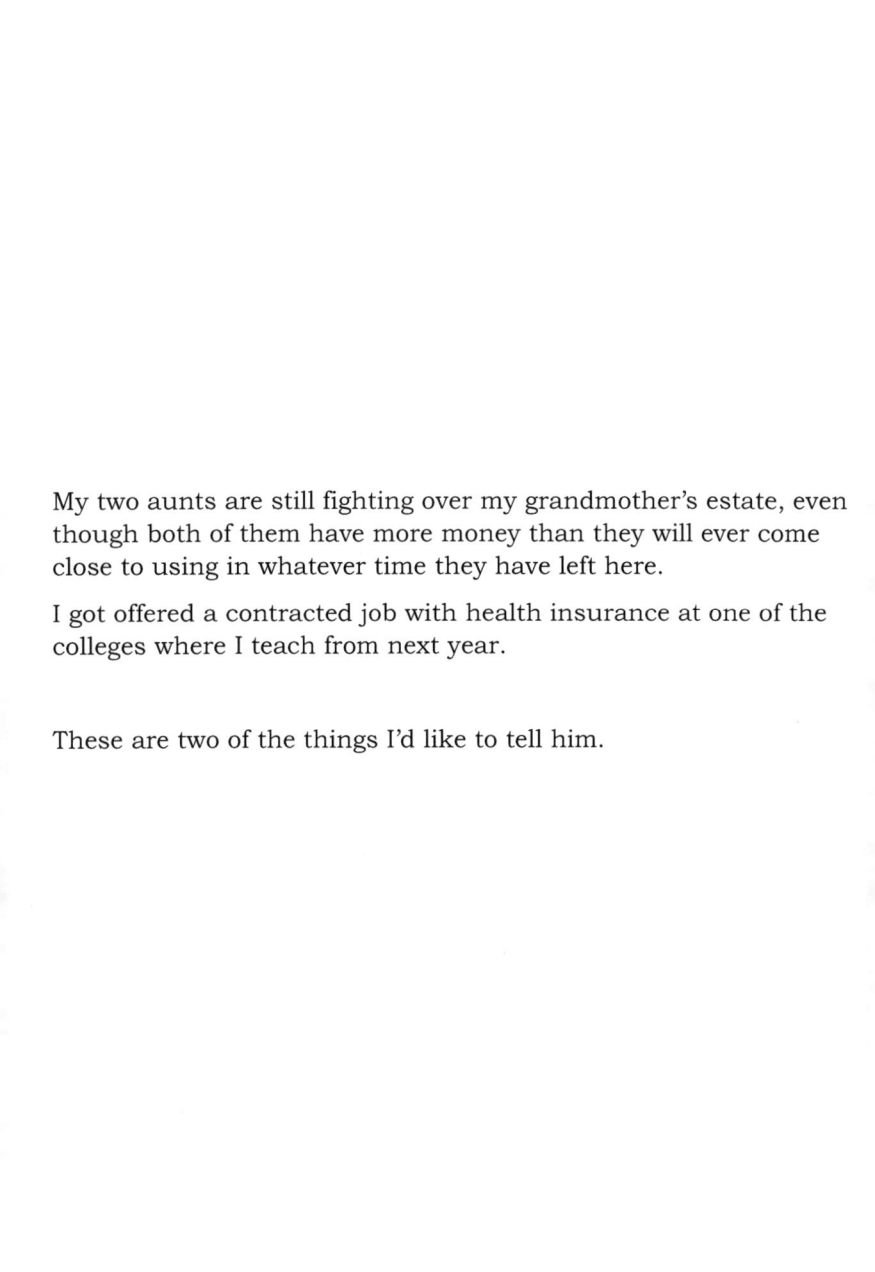

My two aunts are still fighting over my grandmother's estate, even though both of them have more money than they will ever come close to using in whatever time they have left here.

I got offered a contracted job with health insurance at one of the colleges where I teach from next year.

These are two of the things I'd like to tell him.

Back in civilization, New York has a cold. This happens a few times a year. Everyone on the subway is coughing and sniffling.

"It's because of the change in temperature," people say.

No. It's because our immune systems are compromised by a poor diet and a poor sleep cycle. It's because public transportation is a literal Petri dish of bacteria and germs. It's because people hold the pole on the subway and then eat, and then hold the pole again. It's because people hold the pole on the subway and then blow their noses, and then hold the pole again. It's because people hold the pole on the subway and then use their phone, rubbing their fingers, ears, mouths, and faces against the screen. And how often do you sanitize your cell phone?

I have the sniffles, too. But it's ok. I'll get over it. This time. And probably the next time, too. And the time after that.

Until one time I won't.

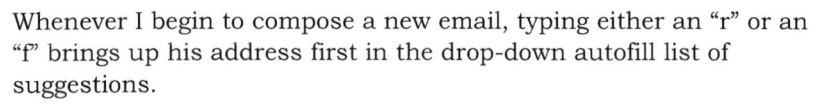

Whenever I begin to compose a new email, typing either an "r" or an "f" brings up his address first in the drop-down autofill list of suggestions.

How long will it be until he is no longer my most-frequently emailed "r"? Or "f"?

Gmail doesn't have a "disable due to death" feature on its autofill. I mean, I suppose I could delete his contact details from my address book. But that would seem more the spiteful reaction of a jilted lover than that of an adult orphaned child.

There was a winter, 9 years ago, when I had pneumonia and was convinced that I had lung cancer when the pleurisy wouldn't subside (so convinced that I pushed things to the point of getting an MRI), a wild, irrational self-diagnosis that just might have been influenced by the fact that I had recently read of the very untimely demise of a kid I knew tangentially at college who had recently died of lung cancer which had initially presented itself as pneumonia which would not abate.

Should I be "proud" of the fact that, at 42, I've already beaten lung cancer, mouth cancer (don't ask), and HIV (really, don't ask)?

And yet my father had a heart attack and a triple bypass at 36, a double knee replacement in his mid-50s, shoulder surgery, wrist surgery, a defibrillator, and two cornea replacements.

So it is safe to say that my hypochondria is not an inherited trait – my mother got sick once, and it was cancer, and she died. My father endured pretty much everything hypochondriacs worry about having, and moved through each malady with resolution and minimal existential reflection.

Maybe they were just of a different generation.

Or maybe I'm a fucking pussy.

But really, you could die *now*. Literally, right now. You could get hit by a car, or killed in a rampage shooting, or felled by an aneurysm. Today.

Or you could go for a check-up, and find out something is growing inside you, something which they can't take out, something which means you only have months to live, and, though you will not die today, life as you have always known it will effectively have ended, insofar as whatever you haven't done yet, you are now not going to do.

Yet even if we become aware of this, we cannot truly act in a concrete, measurable way which would reflect the assimilation of this knowledge. If we go around telling the people who we love that we love them every day, the words quickly lose their potency, and become tantamount to a daily greeting or sign-off phrase signaling the end of phone conversations. If we make an effort to "live life to the fullest," what does that even mean? Lots of GoPro videos of ourselves bungee jumping off bridges in Southeast Asia? An explosion of random physical encounters with a series of people from different walks of life? Increased experimentation with various intoxicants and altered states? (And if here you would say "No, living life to the fullest does not mean casual sex and drug use," the next one or 10 times you hear someone use the phrase, ask yourself if the speaker is referring to the desire to spend his or her life in temperance and moderation, in a loving stable, monogamous partnership, or if really, something closer to the exact opposite is what's being alluded to).

All physical pleasures exist on a sliding scale of diminishing returns. But you can't know that until you place yourself somewhere on that scale and begin the descent.

Perhaps the best we can do is appreciate things more (witness the meteoric rise in "mindfulness" as mantra and mission statement). And perhaps, to return to the ostensible focus of this text, that's what my father did.

He was not stupid, but he was no existentialist, and unless he kept it very quiet, he seemed largely unburdened by metaphysical quandaries.

Is *that* a lesson I should have heeded better from the example of his life?

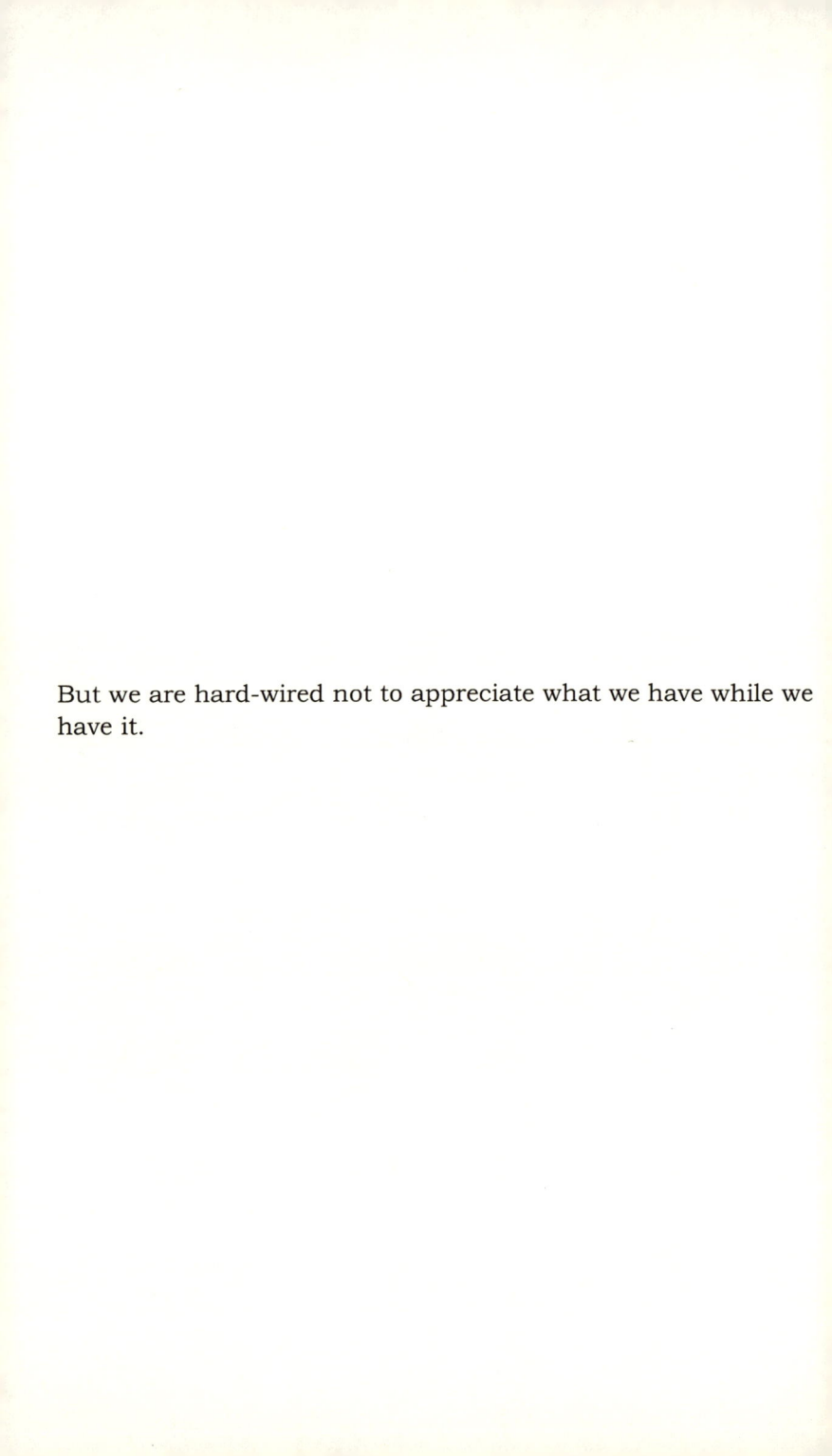

But we are hard-wired not to appreciate what we have while we have it.

Halfway through my 43rd year here, I have no parents, no siblings, no children, no spouse. I have currently been single for over 8 years.

It would be neither unfair nor incorrect to say that I am not profoundly connected to Life. It would not be inaccurate to say that there are days on which I cannot convincingly claim that the benefits of sustaining this human existence measurably outweigh embracing the possible alternative.

Fortunately, decisiveness, among many, many other things, has never been my strong point.

And really, though, killing myself at this point would seem somewhat redundant.

At some stage in life you realize that you shouldn't care so much about the little things. Then later on, you realize that *all things* are little.

If I died tomorrow, not only would it not really matter to anyone, there would not even be anyone I could reasonably expect to be responsible for organizing my funeral.

I would say "And I wonder why I'm so much fun at parties," but I don't get invited to many parties anymore.

But perhaps such reflections do not belong here. Because most of these sentiments existed long before my father no longer did.

Most of them have very little to do with him.

There I go again, making this about myself.

"I'd like to call my father today." -

This thought comes to me unburdened as I walk near Union Square on a rainy afternoon.

"You can't – he's dead."

The idea which follows it into my conscious.

Grief is so non-linear that it is even possible to lose one's place in one's own process of mourning.

Still trying to get comfortable with the concept of "forever".

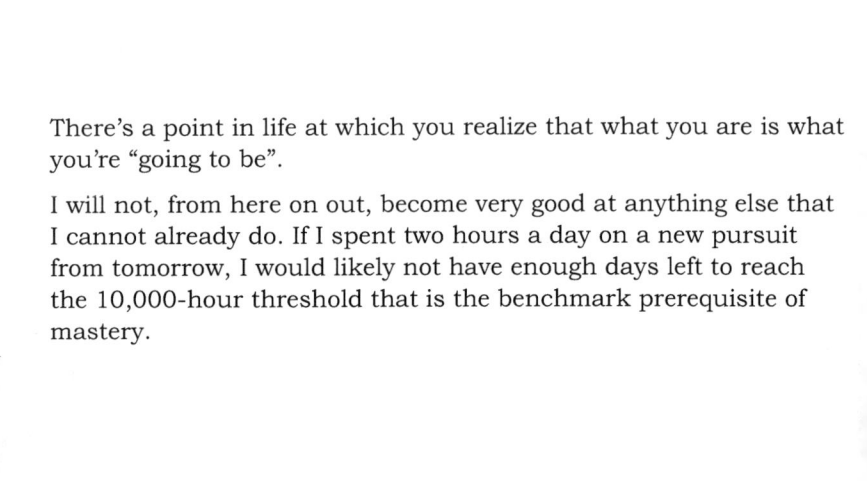

There's a point in life at which you realize that what you are is what you're "going to be".

I will not, from here on out, become very good at anything else that I cannot already do. If I spent two hours a day on a new pursuit from tomorrow, I would likely not have enough days left to reach the 10,000-hour threshold that is the benchmark prerequisite of mastery.

And by the time you realize that there's a finite point in life from which you can realistically no longer "be whatever you want to be", that point has probably long since passed.

There have been psychological studies which have asked participants to hypothesize about their mood and level of life satisfaction after significant positive and negative events. In one, participants were asked, "How do you think you would feel after winning a lottery jackpot?" versus, "How do you think you would feel after being in an accident which paralyzed you for life?"

Of course, people imagining themselves winning the lottery think that their post-victory existence will be a dream. And those projecting themselves confined to a wheelchair cannot imagine that they'd even have the strength to go on.

But when comparing these hypothetical responses to people who actually won the lottery, and to people who actually were in accidents which resulted in a loss of mobility, what researchers found was that in both groups, general self-reported levels of life satisfaction weren't all that different than they had been before the "life-altering" event.

We are very bad at imagining how something would make us feel. We are very bad at knowing what would make us happy. And really, almost anything that happens to us, good or bad, doesn't change us all that much for all that long.

Your grief in a period of mourning has very much to do with you, and very little to do with the person who's gone. After all, at this point, they aren't doing very much of anything.

He's gone, but I've still got to go to work next week. I've still got to pay rent on the 1st of the month. I've still got to figure out what to do with the few decades of life I've possibly got left.

These things all matter a lot, but also, not very much at all.

I was born with a congenital heart defect which almost required open heart surgery and quite likely could have killed me before my first birthday.

I almost drowned when I was 4 or 5, at the beach, falling off the back of a family friend who would, himself, be lost in a car accident shortly after.

I had tickets flying out of Newark Airport on September 12, 2001.

I came very close, two years back, to sliding clear off a mountain in Central Chile.

Shit, four months ago, I'm pretty certain I took the downtown "A" train directly before one that derailed and caught on fire.

Life is just a series of bad things that almost happen to you. Until one does.

The last time he took me to the airport at the start of an international job assignment was last September, when I went off to Iraq. We got to the airport early, like we usually did. We sat at a table in a food court for a while, and I cried, a little, as did he. There were so many of these departures that it would not be incorrect to say that a large portion of the most meaningful exchanges that he and I shared in my "adult" years were set against a backdrop of departure announcements in Newark or JFK.

"I don't know how many more of these I have in me," he said to me, and I told him I didn't know how many more of them I was planning to undertake, either. I wasn't sure if he meant emotionally, or physically, as his body was failing on various levels, in varying degrees of severity. He told me he'd told his wife not even to tell me if something bad happened to him while I was gone, because he wouldn't want me to bother coming home. He said it not looking to make me feel guilty, but simply because it seemed pragmatic.

He asked how I thought it had affected me, all of the migration, 9 international moves in 20 years. I paused for a moment, before answering, and told him, "I leave people so they can't leave me. I leave people before they can leave me. I have done this so many times that it is far more than a habit – it is a way of life, the only one I know." I started to cry, then, and he patted me on the hand I'd placed on the table between us, which, for us, was a good amount of physical contact.

"Is that all?" he asked.

"Isn't that *enough*?" I replied.

Stop. This isn't about You, man.

But there is no right or wrong way to grieve.

Three weeks After, there is still a message on my voicemail from his wife, the one she left That Morning. She called while I was in the shower, and when I did not answer, she called again.

The message is 10 seconds long.

I cannot answer it.

I cannot erase it.

Also, I've been bumping into people on purpose. One thing I can't handle is when people enter a crowded train and then just plant themselves in the doorway. I push a woman out of the way an hour before the afternoon rush, and when she says, "Say 'excuse me'!" I just shrug, and say, frowning theatrically, "Yeah, you got me."

She then begins to curse me out, loud and long, insulting my manhood, my decency, my humanity, while I stand five feet away, reading a book.

I move to the next train car when we reach the next stop.

I don't know what I want right now, but I don't want this.

Maybe this is the point at which people start looking for a fight club.

I am Jack's grieving nightmare.

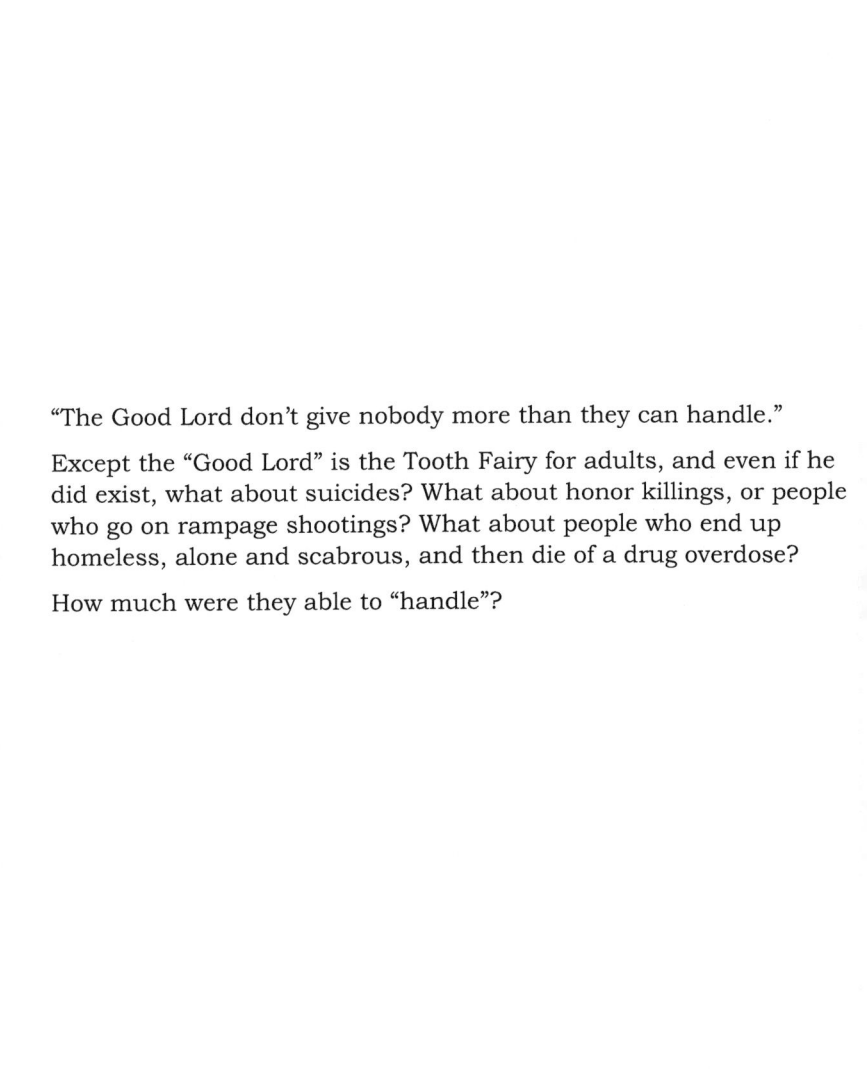

"The Good Lord don't give nobody more than they can handle."

Except the "Good Lord" is the Tooth Fairy for adults, and even if he did exist, what about suicides? What about honor killings, or people who go on rampage shootings? What about people who end up homeless, alone and scabrous, and then die of a drug overdose?

How much were they able to "handle"?

Of an afternoon, I'm teaching a class on how to say different types of numbers in English. It's actually a fun lesson, because generally students learning the language think once they can count to a hundred, they're good. But what about fractions? Decimals? Big numbers that aren't round?

I use a website which takes statistics and crunches the numbers so that it keeps a running "real-time" tally of things like the world's population, global expenditures on various things, and how many cell phones have been sold/cigarettes smoked/emails sent today.

One of the first numbers to appear on the list is "deaths in the world today". As I focus the class on the screen, getting them to practice saying the different numbers that appear, the death tally creeps towards 93,000. It is 1.30PM, and nearly 100,000 people have already died today. That's 100,000 families grieving. That's at least several hundred thousand people who are saddened by someone's passing. *Today.*

I'm three weeks further removed from the death I experienced than these people are. And I'm sure many of them are far less capable of managing their loss.

Even in mourning, you are nothing special.

I stopped smoking over a year ago - it's just the occasional green cookie now to get high. The last time I even did that was the night before he died, alone in my apartment, tweaking out and bingeing a series I already can't remember the name of. The cookie that night was strong enough to make me jittery, and, for a brief moment (which now seems ironic), feel as though I might be at risk of a heart attack.

Now, on the five-year anniversary of Hurricane Sandy's landfall, I get high for the first time since he's gone. The day, already grey and untoward, takes on an oneiric feel, a lambent hue, as I lose myself in the afternoon walking around midtown.

At some point it begins to feel unreal, in a very literal sense. Partially it's because I'm high, and partially it's because that's what everyone says after a loved one is gone. And it *shouldn't* feel real, because it's never been that way in your entire life up until this point. You don't lose someone for a while, then have them come back, then lose them again.

However, at the moment, it feels so *not* real that it almost strikes me as some elaborate performance art piece, the last month. Like I want to take out my phone and call him and, when he answers, say, "You old bastard, I knew you weren't *really* dead. How are you?"

At some point, walking down 6th Avenue, I find myself in conversation with him.

"It's rough," I tell him. "What do you want me to say?"

"I don't' know," he answers, "How are you dealing with it?"

"Well, we weren't all that actively a part of each other's lives, you know, so the day-to-day is pretty much the same."

"Yeah," he concedes.

"But don't think that that means this hasn't affected me," I rush to say, "I mean, I'm *human*. It's strange. It's, just, a lot to handle."

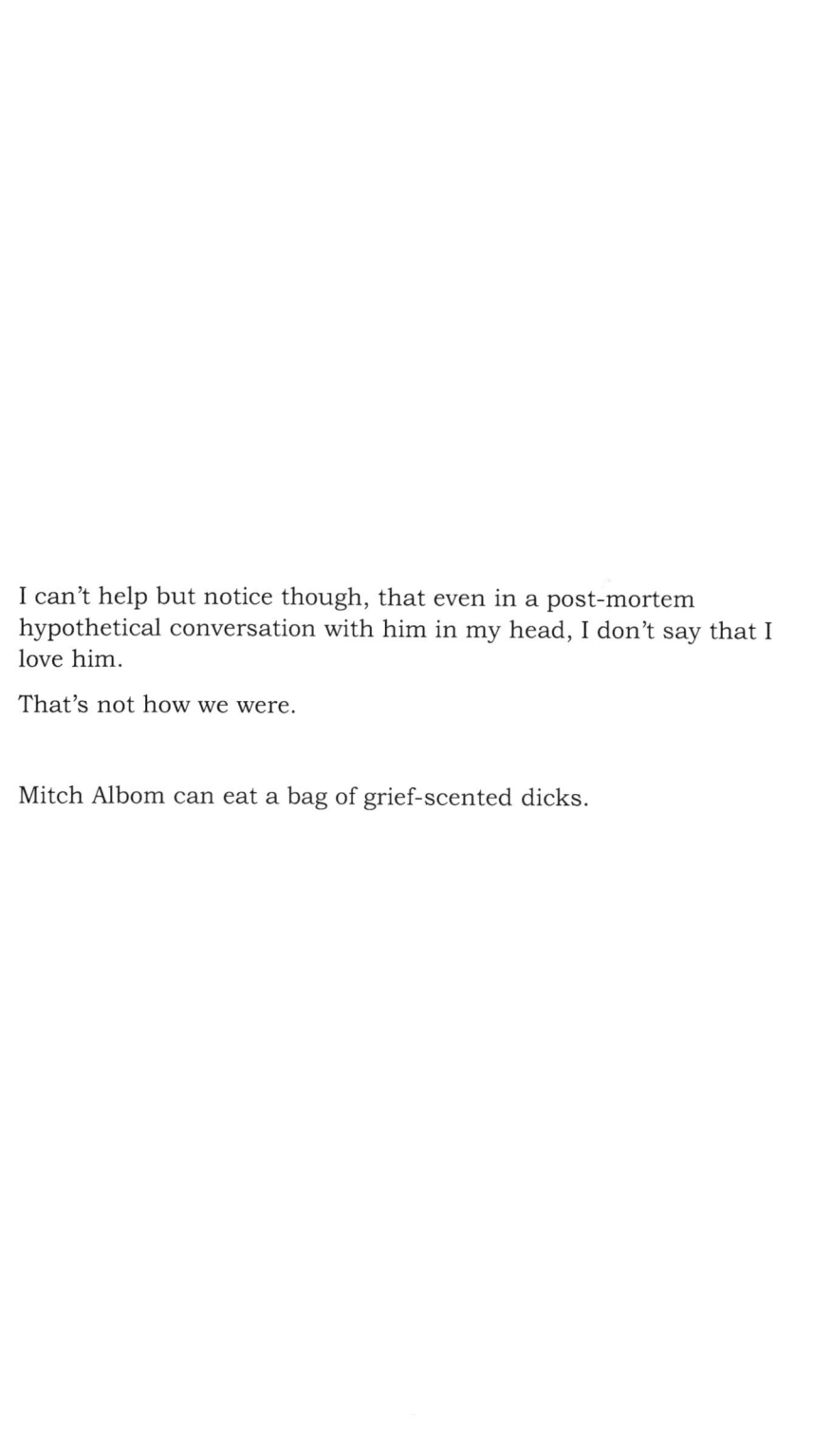

I can't help but notice though, that even in a post-mortem hypothetical conversation with him in my head, I don't say that I love him.

That's not how we were.

Mitch Albom can eat a bag of grief-scented dicks.

"There's police everywhere downtown," I hear a man say calmly into his phone as I walk south down 8th Avenue in Chelsea. And I know again that it's terrorism before even looking online to confirm it.

We have grown so comfortable with this now that we no longer realize how strange it is that it isn't strange.

Eight dead, hit and hit and hit and don't really even run.

This is where I'd get a message from him, wondering if I was ok. Or where I'd preemptively send him one just to let him know that I was.

Instead, I get a message from his wife. "Still alive," I respond.

"That's good," she says. "So am I."

It either happens suddenly, or it doesn't. A heart attack, a stroke, a car accident.

Or, cancer. MS. Alzheimer's.

You're either prepared, or you aren't. You've got a valid will, you've shared what you wanted to with your loved ones, you've crossed as much off the bucket list as you could reasonably have been expected to.

Or you haven't.

I already have a will. I don't have many loved ones. And I've been crossing things off my bucket list for the past two decades.

But I still don't think I'm ready to go.

Not just yet.

How many years do I have left? 10? 15? 30?

How many *good* years do I have left? A handful? None?

The human brain does not possess the capacity to adequately or accurately conceive of the passing of time, either in retrospect or going forward. If someone told me today that I have 15 years left to live, I would feel that to be a horribly short time. But if you asked me to think about where I was 15 years ago, and to consider all that's happened between then and now, it feels as though several lifetimes have passed.

Or 20 minutes.

Or both.

There is no correct way to apprehend the passing of time. It passes; it is unrecoverable. You were there, and now you are here, and later you will be gone.

And someone will attempt to eulogize you in 500 words or less.

If you're lucky.

And these thoughts, these ruminations, these concerns and conjectures, are all worn paths. Nothing you can say, or do, or feel in these moments, in this period, has not been said, or done, or felt, across the millennia, by countless others. The wrought hands, the imprecations, the Kubler-Rossian staging of it all. You didn't invent this shit. You don't own it.

In fact, the only unique element or aspect of your grief, literally the only one, is that you are experiencing it in the first person.

I wonder what it felt like. That's what I'd like to ask him. Though he had his first heart attack in 1983, and I had 34 years to ask him about that one and never did.

But it's not the pain I'm curious about. It's how long he was aware enough to realize what was happening. It's what he thought about in those final moments.

Was he afraid? At peace? Angry?

It doesn't make a difference if someone is holding your hand. We all die alone.

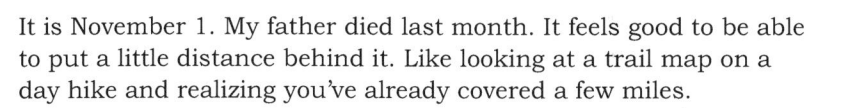

It is November 1. My father died last month. It feels good to be able to put a little distance behind it. Like looking at a trail map on a day hike and realizing you've already covered a few miles.

There are still many friends in other time zones who do not know, friends with whom I have chatted online over the course of the past month, about other things. Friends who did not ask "How are you?" because online conversations are often asynchronous and non-linear. Someone sends a link, someone responds. A GIF. A meme. "My father died" would just spoil the mood.

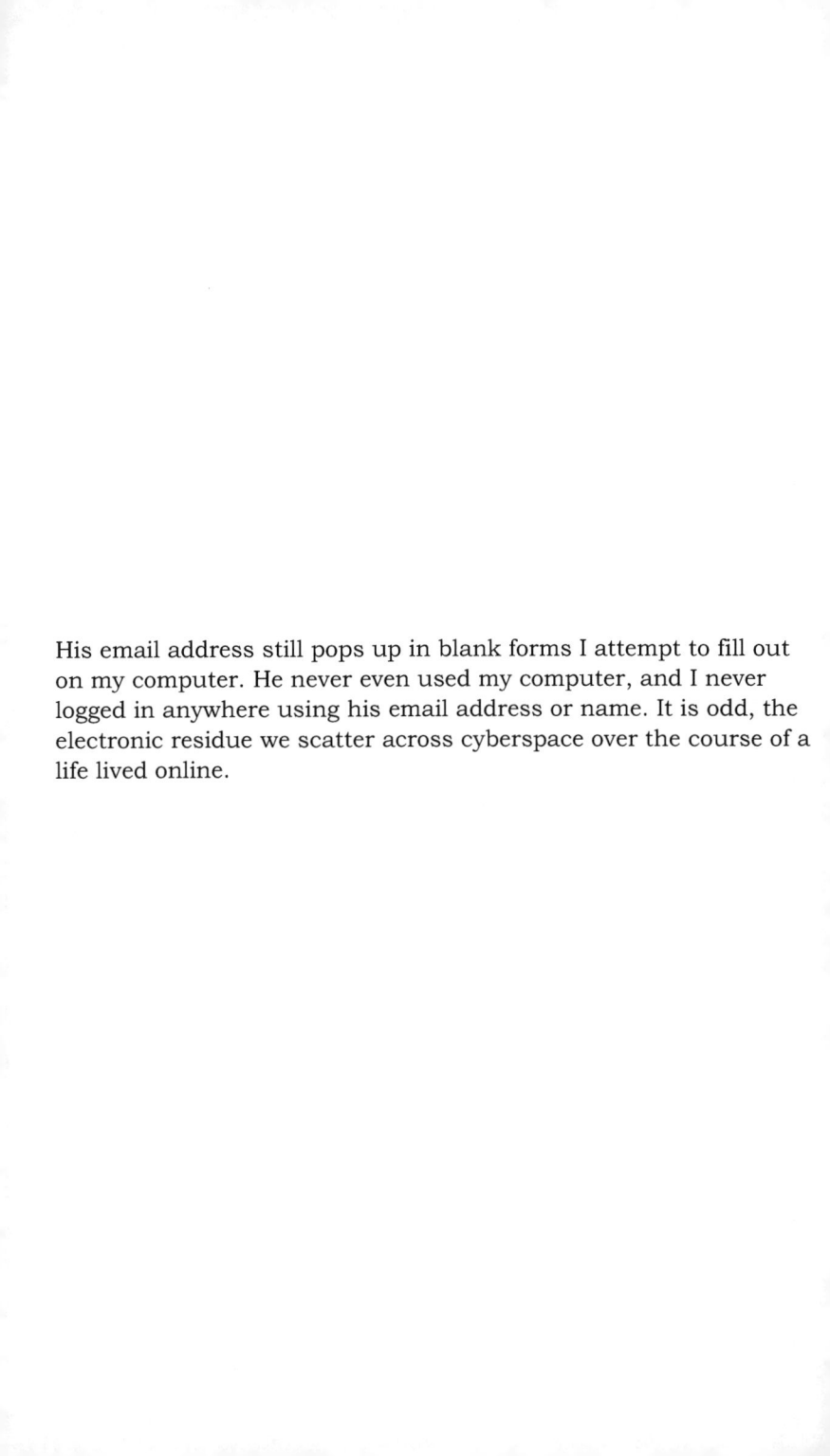

His email address still pops up in blank forms I attempt to fill out on my computer. He never even used my computer, and I never logged in anywhere using his email address or name. It is odd, the electronic residue we scatter across cyberspace over the course of a life lived online.

Sometimes, though, life just beats you over the head with it.

The series my high school friend created, which I binge one afternoon to catch up with, seems obsessed with the theme of dying fathers. The overarching plotline of the first 1.5 seasons has been a slow reveal of the details of the death of the patriarch. A subplot – a middle-aged man reunites with his long-lost father, a man who abandoned him at birth. They make amends before the father dies. A new plotline hinted at – the death of the father of the patriarch, and how that affected him.

A sentence in a grammar book I'm teaching from in a lesson on adjective clauses: "A father is a person whose_____".

The title of a chapter in a novel another class has been assigned is literally just *"Dead Father"*.

I'd like to think maybe he would have laughed at this, at least a bit.

I mean, what's the alternative?

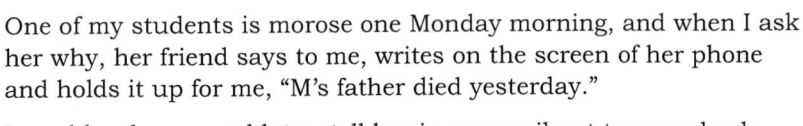

One of my students is morose one Monday morning, and when I ask her why, her friend says to me, writes on the screen of her phone and holds it up for me, "M's father died yesterday."

I send her home, and later, tell her in an email not to come back until she is ready, and that I don't care if she's on a student visa which requires her attendance in class. "I'll mark you as present, and if INS has a problem, they can come and talk to me," I tell her.

It's funny, the things you regret.

There was a time, when I was living in Spain, and high, basically, all the time. It was after 9/11, when, for the first time, I realized I was actively avoiding my country of birth.

It must have been 2002, 2003, because I had discovered illegal downloading of music and had told him about it. We weren't sharing much of anything at that point, and he asked me if I could download a CD for him. I don't remember which.

Instead of just doing it and mailing it to him, I sent him instructions on how to download the program I used to download things. I doubt the instructions were even good. It would have been like explaining to someone who's never made toast how to prepare turducken.

"If you can't do it, that's ok," he said. And the fact that I still remember this exchange 15 years on probably means something, though I'm not sure exactly what.

On a Bronx-bound D train, a kid of about 15 is having a fairly mature discussion about politics with his father. The father is the age that Manhattan fathers of 15-year olds now are, which is to say, his mid-fifties. The kid keeps talking over the father, arguing the position that a fact can be what you feel, and his fundamental misunderstanding of the meaning of the word is matched at each exchange by his agitated insistence.

After being cut off for the third or fourth time, the father finally says to him, politely, softly, and deferentially, "Would you please let me finish my statement first?"

At this, the kid actually steps back a bit and replies, "I feel like you're being really aggressive right now."

Is it ok to hit someone else's kid? What if the parent himself would high-five you after you did it?

Is this kid how I was at that age?

No. I wouldn't have couched my defiance in pop psychology jargon.

Is the dad the way my father was at that age?

No. He would have ended the discussion several exchanges earlier, if he'd even endeavored to debate me at all.

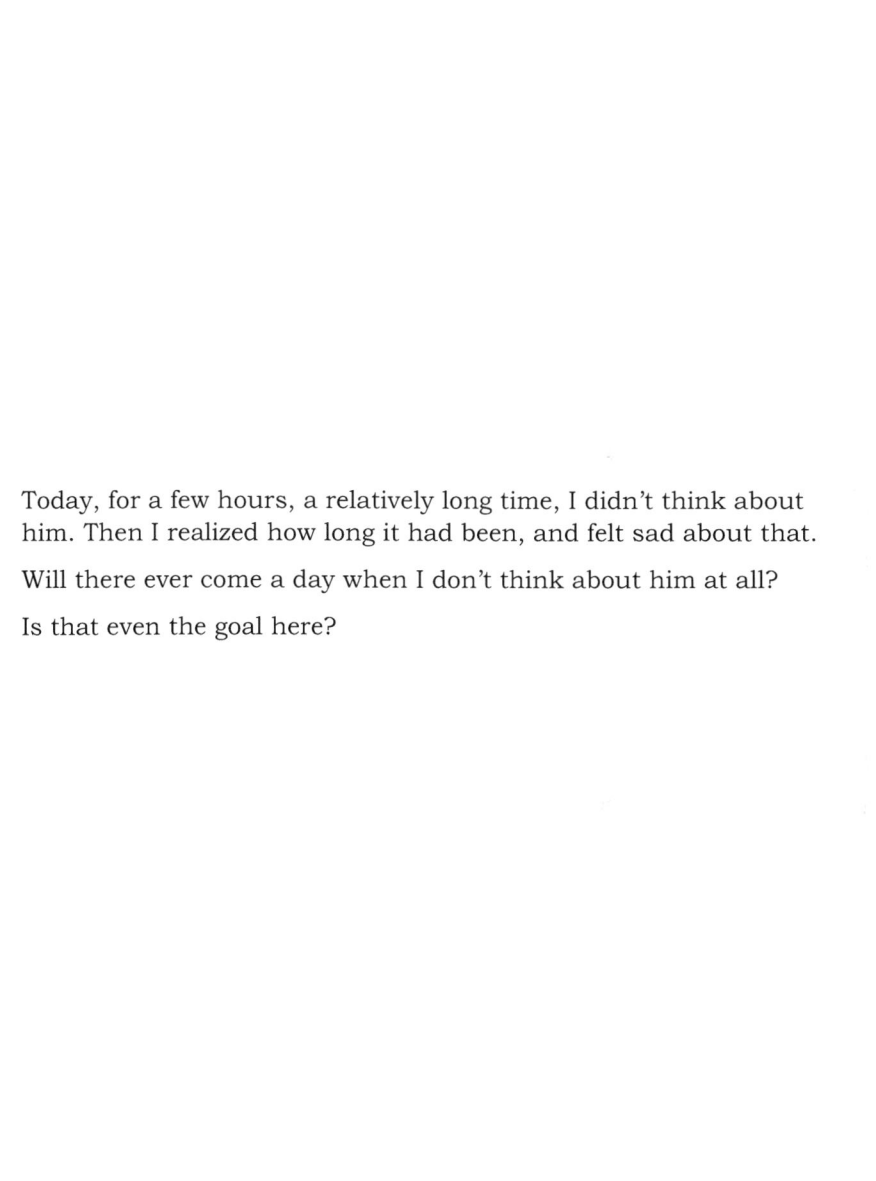

Today, for a few hours, a relatively long time, I didn't think about him. Then I realized how long it had been, and felt sad about that.

Will there ever come a day when I don't think about him at all?

Is that even the goal here?

Also, everyone is a sexual predator. That happens over the course of a few short weeks. I wonder what he would feel about this. I wonder what *I* feel about this. I wonder how you "should" feel when your hero turns out to have been a very bad person in his private life.

One of the few real cultural pleasures I give my father credit for having introduced me to is Louis CK. I mean, I would have found out about him anyway, but I definitely remember him telling me, "Check this guy out!" a dozen or so years ago.

I'd really like to talk to him about this. In a way, it feels like yet another death, because, while Louis the man is not technically gone, there will be no more comedy coming from him for a very long time, if ever. It will most likely become unacceptable in most social circles to even admit that you still find him funny.

But I do. And I will.

What do we require of the people who entertain us? To what extent does their character matter?

Does jerking off in front of a few women who didn't want to see that, and asking a few others if you could, and then not jerking off when they said "Please don't" make you a monster? Or does it just make you a weird, sad pervert? Does it make the fact that you have been very funny for a very long time now, somehow, not "count"?

And due to the unfortunate timing of it, history is going to lump him in with Harvey Weinstein, and Kevin Spacey, and Woody Allen, and whatever other rapists, presumed or verifiable, are outed by the time you finish reading this sentence. And it doesn't seem fair. It wasn't fair to the women Louis harassed, but it's also not fair to the millions of people who use his standup as therapy.

In fact, following a strict line of utilitarian ethics, you could argue that the discomfort suffered by those women does not, in fact, outweigh the pleasure experienced by the millions of fans that he has, and so, the actual *morally correct* response in this situation, following the Greatest Happiness Principle, would be to let him keep on acting, producing, and doing comedy, even if it means he has to jerk off to completion in someone's unwilling presence every once in a while.

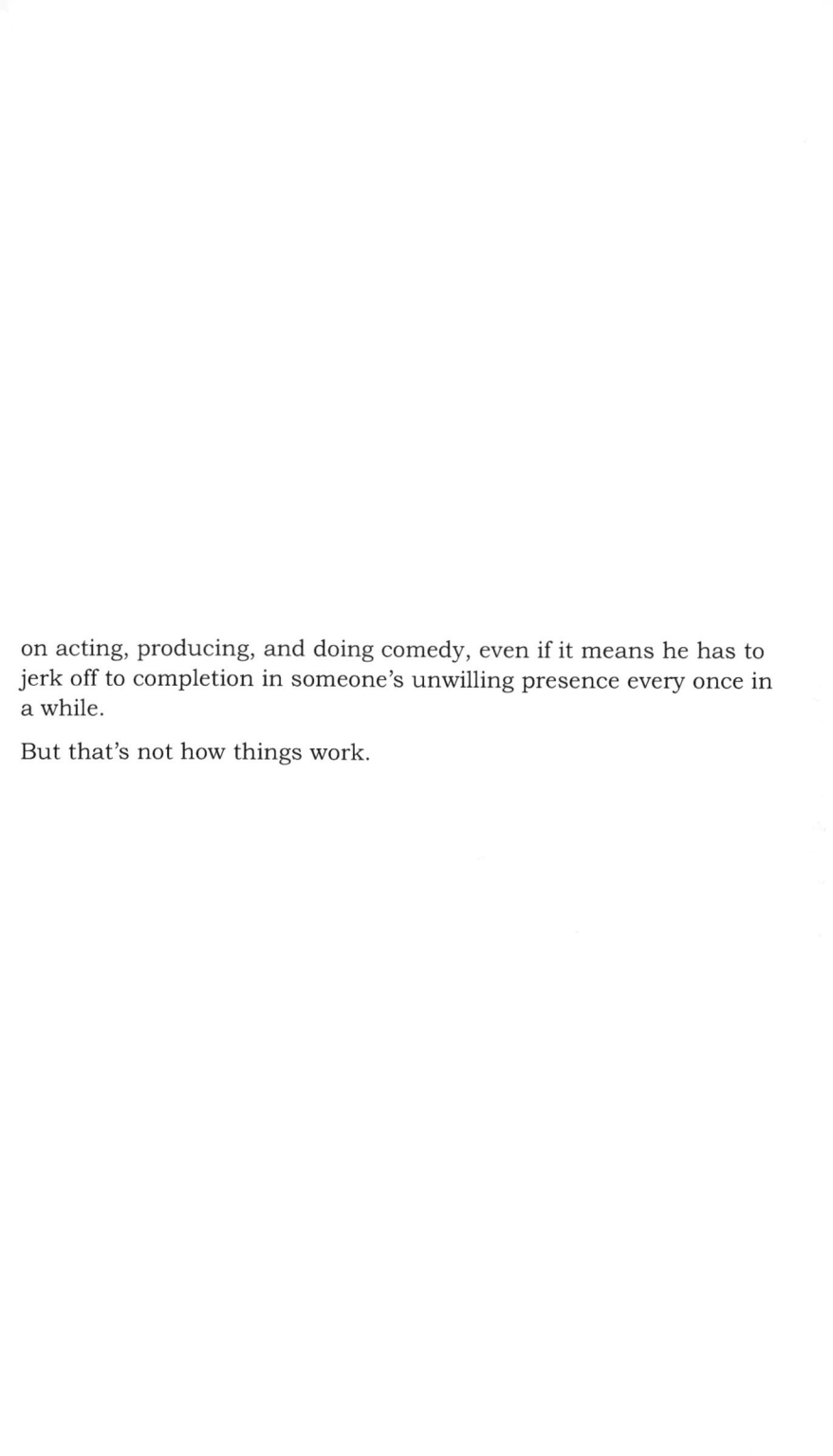

But that's not how things work.

I receive an email, addressed to seven people, from the therapist who is running a new bereavement group which I've decided to attend. He asks us to email the name of the deceased, the date of death, and our age and occupation. I feel the need to qualify the relatively recent date of his death by saying "but he had several serious health issues, so it wasn't entirely unexpected."

I'm sure I will be judged for adding this. I'm sure I will be judged for everything I say in the group. Just as surely, I will be judging everyone else's statements in the sessions. I don't know if I need to pay $60 to judge and be judged for 90 minutes a week. I don't know if I will be farther along the road to recovery than the others in the group. I know it's not a competition, but in all likelihood, I'll be treating it as such.

Maybe my baseline was so low that it's not that hard to get back to it.

"And would you like to elaborate on that?"

"Fuck you. There's your elaboration."

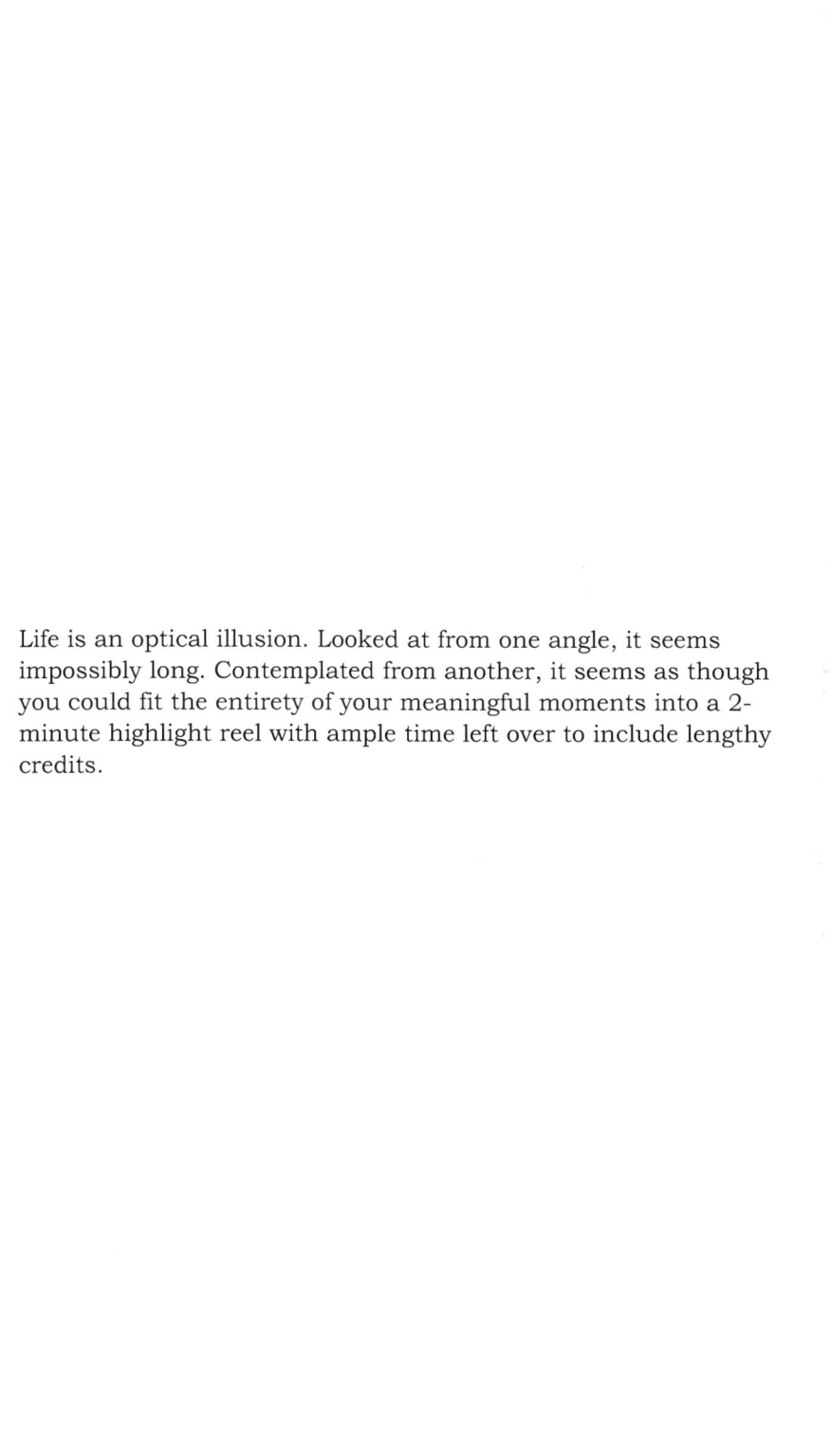

Life is an optical illusion. Looked at from one angle, it seems impossibly long. Contemplated from another, it seems as though you could fit the entirety of your meaningful moments into a 2-minute highlight reel with ample time left over to include lengthy credits.

At 8, I was a scrawny, frightened ball of nerves who would cry before school every day and often woke with a pain in my stomach which radiated all the way down until it convulsed my sphincter. I was scared of everything, willing to try nothing.

At 18, I was a lanky, teetotalling, God-fearing weekly churchgoer who had yet to kiss a girl or develop a personality. I liked what other people liked, except when I didn't, and then only to be contrarian. I did not have a passport. Taco Bell was perhaps my favorite restaurant.

At 28, I was a pill-selling, rave organizing DJ in Barcelona, an illegal immigrant who taught 12 hours a week and chain-smoked hash joints. I regularly spent the majority of calendar years out of the country of my birth. I was several years into semi-vegetarianism, and I was a grudging (at best) agnostic.

At 38, I was a militant atheist university professor with a semi-severe cocaine problem who spent most nights alone in a penthouse apartment overlooking a highway in Bogota. I had already retired from the social side of the party scene, yet still maintained the worst of its vices.

And still we dare extrapolate regarding the path that we will follow in life, confident in the knowledge that we know where we are going.

Many of us move through our time here with all of the direction and logic of a fallen leaf in a gust of wind. A numbered ball in a Bingo drum. All the while, trying to ascribe meaning to our migrations. All the while, looking for a through-line.

I head out to New Jersey to have lunch with his wife. It still feels odd to take a bus through the Lincoln Tunnel and come out on the other side without him waiting for me in a parking lot, angry that I was 10 minutes later than I said I'd be.

We eat. She tells me things about her origin story I never thought to ask. Perhaps each of us is only intrigued by the other's presence because of the connection we represent to him. I have his sense of humor; she knows things about him I wouldn't have ever known. The conversation is easy in a way his and mine never were, which makes me sad on various levels.

Afterwards, we go shopping for a winter coat, because it is winter now, at least for today. I buy an ugly Christmas sweater with a large iron-on patch of a drunk Jesus wearing a "Happy Birthday" hat. "He would have loved that," she says.

There will be a lot of things he would have loved.

I go to a dermatologist to have a persistent discoloration on my ankles checked. His ankles looked like this years ago, when the diabetes was relatively new and hadn't yet begun to shut down his body, bit by bit. Before the neuropathy took away the sensation in both of his feet, and the discoloration deepened and spread all the way up past his knees.

I showed my ankles to him a few months ago, and he said, "That's exactly what happened to me." He said, "I had diabetes a long time before I knew it." He said, "You have to change your diet."

And it's not that I'm not going to get diabetes – statistically speaking, 40% of Americans in my age cohort will. But I had my A1C checked twice this year, and both times the results were within the normal range.

When I was down in Mexico in two months ago, I went to a dermatologist, because there, paying out of pocket is cheaper than the co-pay would be here. She told me it had something to do with broken capillaries, from spending too much time on my feet, or just from bad luck. She told me there was nothing that really could, nor needed to be, done. It is what it is.

By this point, there are already things that aren't worth fixing.

A comedian whose jokes it is no longer acceptable to admit finding funny had a good bit about this.

The dermatologist gave me a prescription for a cortisone cream which I filled and then never used.

When I got back, I told my father about what she'd said, and he told me dismissively, "That's worthless. That doesn't mean anything."

For once, I did not take the bait. "Ok," I said, and changed the topic.

It was, maybe, the last thing we argued about.

The dermatologist in New York takes one look at my ankles and says pretty much the exact same thing as the one in Mexico did. It's something related to capillaries, something that sometimes takes months to resolve. She, too, prescribes a cream for me. She brushes aside my fear that it could be any one of the several life-ending diseases that I Googled it to be. "Come back in three months," she says. "If you want."

Take *that*, Dad.

To celebrate not having diabetes yet, I go and have dinner at an expensive burger place on the Upper West Side, around the corner from the doctor's office. I get a turkey burger and feel completely underwhelmed. This has happened the last few times I've gotten turkey burgers, yet I continue to order them in burger joints. "Why do you get turkey burgers?" he asked me not too long ago. "Even a good one isn't all that good."

You may have had a point there, Old Man.

On balance, each of us was right sometimes, and wrong at others. Each of us made some good points.

But neither of us conceded much.

There are still friends I haven't said anything to about him. Online friends, to be sure, but still. I just, *don't* tell them. It's getting easier and easier to say nothing.

It is very easy to return to baseline. It is very easy to overcome someone else's grief. It has already been long enough that I wouldn't be getting much sympathy from anyone I informed at this point.

I've already abandoned the Word document I began in the immediate aftermath of his death, the one titled "Topics of Conversation", in which I listed things I'd liked to have discussed with him.

Because there will be a lot of things. Sports keep happing. News keeps happening. Life keeps happening.

For those of us still here.

I go to the bereavement group. There are seven of us, and the only other man there is a caricature of obesity who thoroughly occupies the sofa he sits on across from me in the small room. 3.5 of the women are quite attractive. Literally everyone but the guy and me bursts into tears within seconds of beginning their monologues, which the therapist asks us all to give at the start of the session. Three of the women refer to their dead mothers as "their best friend". No one there besides me lost their loved one less than four months ago. I go last, and tell my story in a measured tone, because just seeing five other people cry does not make me want to. It has been a little over six weeks now, and I don't know what I'm supposed to feel (though of course, we've been told that there are no right or wrong answers here), but I'm not feeling much of anything right now. I feel bad that I don't feel much of anything, but this is just another group of people who didn't know my father, didn't know the way we related, and clearly had different relationships with their parents than I did with mine.

The guy, who, it turns out, is gay (though this isn't relevant, I suppose), had a mother who was a drug addict. She died of an overdose. He says they fought a lot, but even he manages to say that they were able to relate better during the final few years of her life, talking almost daily.

Even the guy whose mother was a crackhead had a better relationship with his departed than I did with mine.

At one point, the girl sitting to my left expresses her dismay by wringing her hands theatrically and saying, "Now I'm disappointed in *everything*!" It is very, very hard for me not to interject – "Wait, doesn't *everyone always* feel that way?"

As the session is wrapping up, the leader passes out a homework sheet. The first section of the assignment says: "Please write three paragraphs about your loved one beginning with the following sentences: 1) This is who my loved one was to me: 2) This is the legacy my loved one left me: 3) My life now without my loved one is:"

I cannot come back to this group again, because my answers would be:

1) a guy I probably should have known better, but neither of us made that easy.

2) Always order the special.

3) So similar to what it was before that I'm realizing that, although I have probably needed therapy for quite some time now, it is not for bereavement.

As I walk out into the autumn night, I become sad that I'm not sad. It wouldn't be fair of me to continue coming to this group. If there is an inverse relationship between the closeness of the loved one and the perceived distance of the time of their passing, it's feeling now, a lot of the time, like he's been gone for months.

Some children simply do not get along well with their parents. Some children are simply not close with their parents. And in the absences of a truly malicious act by one party perpetrated against the other, the responsibility for this failing is shared.

However, the ratio of responsibility shifts over time. One could argue that it is a parent's job to make sure his or her young or adolescent children like him or her. But as the child arrives at, and moves into, adulthood, the burden of responsibility changes. By the time the child is 40 (and probably a lot earlier, really), s/he bears a disproportionate amount of the blame.

At some point, your problems are your own. At some point, you have to be the bigger person. At some point, it doesn't matter if some petty shit went down three decades ago. At some point, you just sound like a big fucking baby, talking about how daddy neglected you.

Perhaps one of the truest things I said in my eulogy for him was that he and I weren't close because we were too similar in personality and demeanor. A person like me isn't going to get along well with a person like me.

It's not just that I don't like myself; it's that people like me don't like people like me.

What was I saying about not needing therapy?

In a bar on the night I finish teaching a training course for people who want to teach English overseas, I chat with some of my pupils. As the last session had wrapped up a few hours ago, I contemplated confessing to them that it's been a difficult time for me recently because my father died. This morning, when I woke up, I actually planned to do it, as a way of encouraging them to take the plunge and move away, because you don't know how much time you're going to get to do the things you want (but also, contradictorily, as a warning to not stay away from home so long that the people in your life aren't there anymore). But this afternoon, it didn't feel right, so I kept it to myself.

There is a friendly guy from Virginia with a father in North Carolina he hasn't seen in 7 years. "We talk on the phone," the guy says. "We're close – I just don't need to see him."

There is a girl from Pittsburgh who tells us that last year she had pizza, alone, for Thanksgiving. "This year I might get Chinese," she says.

There is a gay guy from North Carolina who is flying to LA tomorrow. "Is your family there?" I ask.

"No," he says, "but that's where Thanksgiving is this year."

We are all misshapen pieces.

Everyone is a special case.

Some people are gone from your life long before they're dead.

I decide to not even bother with the family that I have left this Thanksgiving. The most enjoyable Thanksgivings I've had were with friends in Barcelona and in Bogota. Hell, even the turkey dinner I had at the Hard Rock Café in Tokyo 17 years ago was kind of fun. A story, at least.

I know a couple in Philadelphia who bought a house a little while back and have been inviting me to come down ever since. Even now, when I'm not working, I don't stay in the US, so it's probably a good idea to take advantage of the 5-day weekend to do a little domestic tourism.

On the bus company's website, I find that the most expensive day to buy tickets is not the Wednesday before the holiday. It's not Thursday morning, either. It's Friday. All day on Friday. It's most expensive at the earliest time that you can leave your family without offending anybody.

Family time, for a good chunk of American humanity, is just paying your dues. It's just doing the minimum, so you don't get accused of not. So you don't get written out of any wills.

Not that I ever truly did, but I will never be constrained by even the simplest of familial obligations ever again.

At my first post-family Thanksgiving, the conversation is good, and the food is non-traditional (my semi-serious lamentations on the absence of mashed potatoes and mac and cheese are met with scorn). On Thursday night, the first of two dinners, I am the only person in attendance who grew up in a house where English was the primary language spoken.

On Friday, my friend's siblings turn up with their spouses. Everyone has children, and everyone is happy to see everyone else. No one overuses their smartphone in the company of others. It feels like some odd, *Stepford Wives* alternate universe where conflict does not exist.

It is so foreign to me to be in the presence of a family whose members genuinely enjoy each other's company that I feel like an embedded anthropologist studying the ways and customs of a remote, dying indigenous tribe.

How would it have been had I grown into a family like this?

Would the passing of my father have been sadder, because he would have been that much closer to me, to all of us?

Or would it have been even less turbulent, because a relationship well-formed and well-maintained can be left without regret at any time?

Do the well-adjusted even *grieve* better than the rest of us?

Back in Harlem, my roommate gets an Alexa for his mother's Christmas gift, but sets it up in our apartment for a few days.

It is yet another example of new technology that reminds me I no longer live in the same world as that into which I was born.

Alexa plays music and answers trivia on request. Alexa adds things to your shopping list. Alexa even tells you a joke and sings you a song when you ask it (I do not want to say "her", but it seems unnatural not to).

My roommate says "Alexa, I just farted," and Alexa answers, "Well, it's a good thing I don't have a nose then."

And suddenly, out of nowhere, I am close to tears again. He would have loved this. For 20 minutes, to be sure, because he wouldn't have used it to buy things, or to listen to music, or even to retrieve information. But he would have had a lot of fun with it, at least for a while. I remember how much he liked Furby that year that people liked Furby. I don't even know which country I was in then.

I missed so many things.

And sure, taken individually, most of them didn't mean much. But after a lifetime, those meaningless things add up.

Those meaningless things are pretty much all we have.

Those meaningless things are Life.

Still getting used to the concept of "forever."

Still stumbling over which tense to employ when referring to him.

There is another terrorist attack. I guess it's that time of year. It is either a testament to having been a teacher for too long, or to having been a New Yorker for too long, that my first thought, as I am reading the "Breaking News" on a Monday morning, story still developing, is "How can I connect this to the grammar lesson I have to teach today?"

I text his wife, just to let her know I was not near the Port Authority.

Perhaps it is time to develop a "safe from terrorist attack" autofill template on the Android SMS platform.

Don't worry, Dad – I'm still here.

It has been 10 weeks. I am becoming remarkably adept at caring about unimportant shit again.

It is Christmas. Almost. The best time of the year, the expectancy hanging in the air like so much mistletoe, everyone forced to be just a bit nicer to each other.

I got the check from his estate last week in the mail. It has been sitting under my easy chair, in the envelope it arrived in. For some reason, it feels like cashing it will bring more finality to all of this.

The X dollars won't really change much, one way or the other. It is a check that's large enough to make the teller offer one or another of the bank's horrible investment opportunities to me. It is enough to require a hold for a few days. It is enough for a son who was absent for the majority of his adult life to feel like it could have been less. Or like it could have been more.

It's neither big enough to change things nor small enough to cause offense.

If you think money solves things, talk to someone who has a lot of it. They'll find other things.

It's funny, the times it comes back to you.

I call the storage unit where I keep the life I cannot keep in my apartment to make my monthly payment. This storage unit was one of the last things he and I talked about. It will always be one of the last things he and I talked about. As long as I have this storage unit, the folder in which I keep the contract will be titled "B-Storage" in his handwriting. Although we did not visit it together more than ten times, any time I go to it, for as long as I am renting it, from now on, I will recall him sitting in his car, doing a crossword puzzle, as I played box Tetris or went hunting for very specific needles in my own private haystack, while he pretended not to lose patience.

I have a keychain with his likeness on it from the company he worked for as a salesman for most of my childhood. At some point in the late 70s, it was evidently deemed a prudent use of promotional funds to make plastic keychains in the shape of rotary phone dials with the images of sales reps on them.

I have the fox-hair fox which I brought him back from Japan, which he hung on the rear-view mirror of every car he had for the last 18 years of his life.

The Yankees beanie hasn't been worn since the playoffs ended, because I have 3 beanies I like more than it, and because a 42-year old shouldn't be wearing sports-themed clothing outside of a stadium unless he's coaching the fucking team.

Any way you calculate things, they don't add up to much.

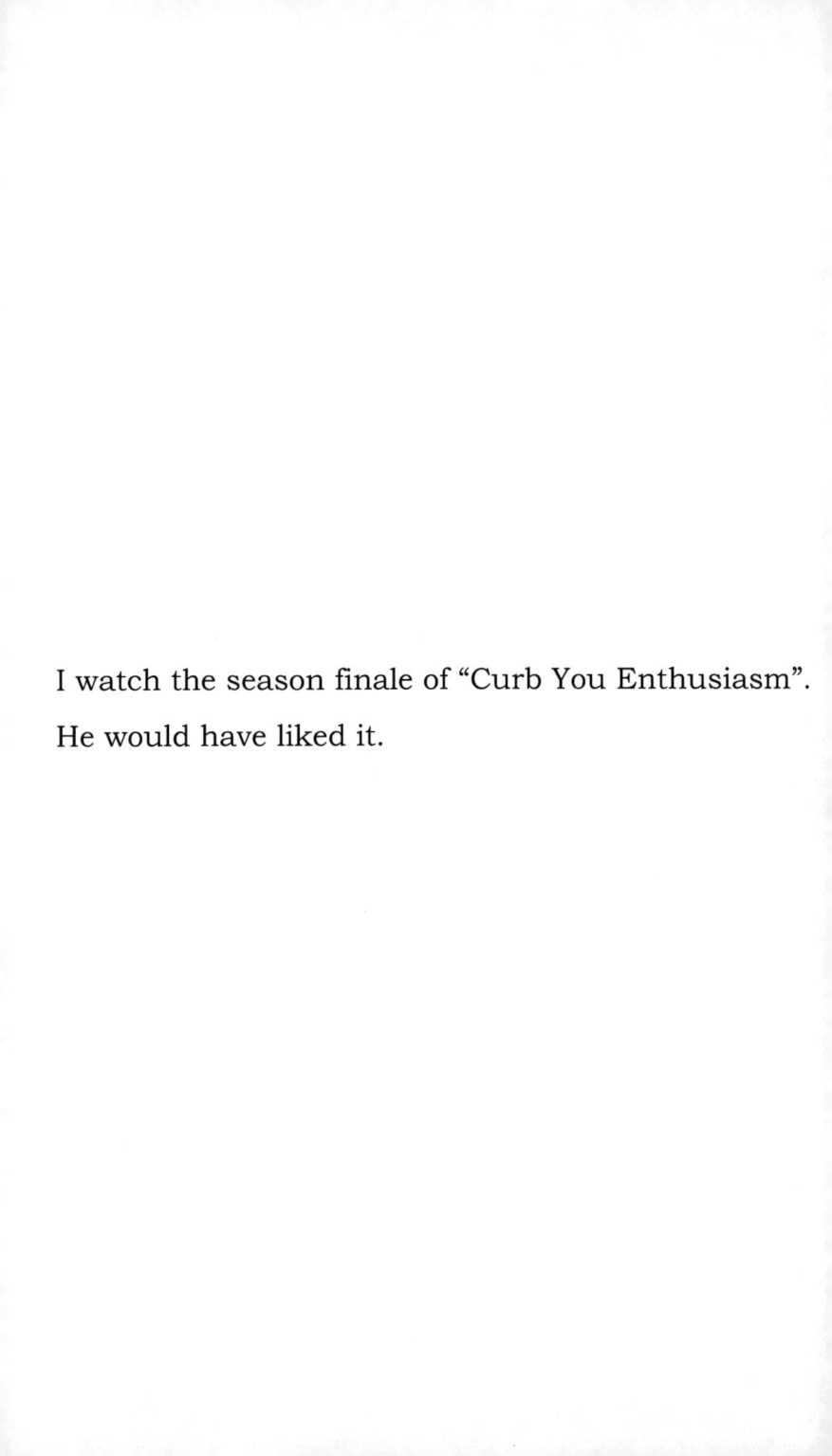

I watch the season finale of "Curb You Enthusiasm". He would have liked it.

It's funny, the things you regret.

When the World Cup came to the US in 1994, I had just graduated high school, and was, for that time, and for my nationality, a big soccer fan. We went to a few games, because you could buy tickets at the box office the day of the match (that's how popular soccer was in the country then).

At a quarterfinal match, between Germany and Bulgaria, we sat down next to a guy who was in his twenties, maybe drunk, and waving a German flag. I don't really remember what happened, but the flag was big, and the guy was not, and it kept hitting us in the face, and my father told him to stop, and I was sitting in between the two of them, a scrawny, scared, 19-year old pussy, and they both got up, and my father pushed the flag away, and then the guy pushed my father, and it didn't amount to more than that, except that my father's sunglasses went flying and had to be handed back to him, and ushers moved the guy to another seat.

If that had happened 10, 15 years later, I would have literally ended up in jail for what I'd have done to the guy.

Sorry, Dad. Again.

At some point, you've already had your last birthday, your last Christmas, your last spring. At some point, you've already seen your last World Cup, your last presidential election.

At some point, you're watching TV series you won't be around to see the end of. The eternal cliffhanger.

And there ain't no Netflix subscription in heaven.

Most of us don't really know when we've reached that point, though.

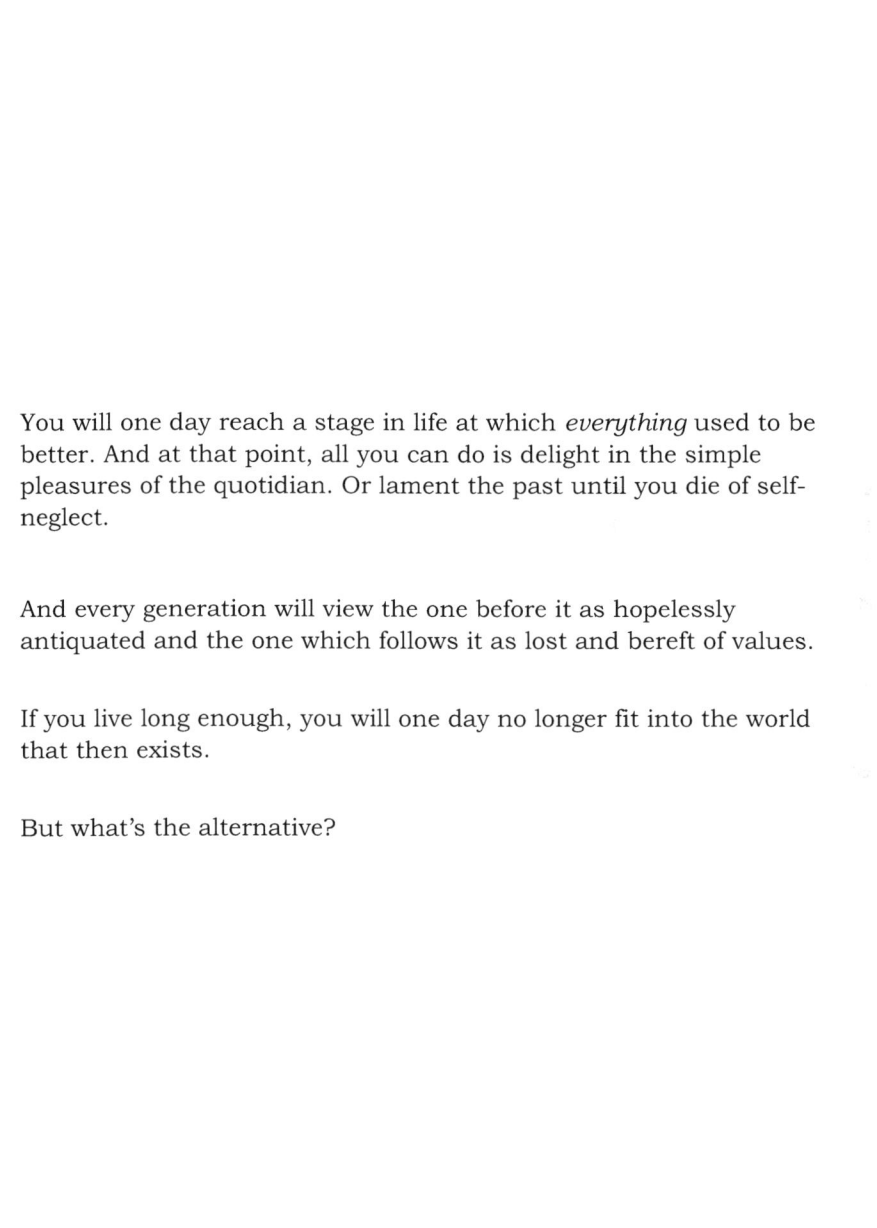

You will one day reach a stage in life at which *everything* used to be better. And at that point, all you can do is delight in the simple pleasures of the quotidian. Or lament the past until you die of self-neglect.

And every generation will view the one before it as hopelessly antiquated and the one which follows it as lost and bereft of values.

If you live long enough, you will one day no longer fit into the world that then exists.

But what's the alternative?

Halfheartedly, I look at positions overseas for the coming year.

I don't have to be here.

But really, I don't have to be anywhere.

And if you keep moving, just for movement's sake, you're always the New Guy. And no one ever really gets to know you.

But if you don't ever let anyone truly get to know you, it's almost like you weren't even here.

And one day soon, one day uncomfortably soon, it will be you in the ground. And it will feel unique, on the way down, because you only live once, and you only die once.

But any realizations or rationalizations you make in that moment will have been made by tens of thousands who have come before you, and by tens of thousands more to come down the line.

If everyone is unique, then no one is.

And you will not be grieved for long by many. And you will be forgotten by virtually everyone in the space of a generation or two. And your possessions certainly won't remember who had them.

The sum total effect of a life, even when contemplated from a relatively short timeline, is shockingly small.

And you can rest easy with this, if you manage to, or you can let it destroy you. Either way, it will happen all the same.

And as this life slowly becomes what is Normal, it's hard to neglect the realization that, for a long time, in my mind, this was going to be The Worst Thing. The phone call I didn't want to receive while living overseas, the loss of the only remaining blood relative who meant very much of anything at all to me. I feared that phone call from more time zones than I could easily count.

And then it happened. And I'm still here. And in the morning, I get up and go to work. And at night, I read a few pages in a book, and I go to sleep. And already, nobody really asks me how I am, or how I feel about what happened.

No one else really cares, because it is so very easy to overcome someone else's grief.

But even for me, now it's just Something That Happened.

And it feels either profoundly, or cripplingly, liberating.

                Is Being really this Unbearably Light?

It is possible, albeit highly unlikely, that I will be able to live as long again without him as I did with him. That would mean I make it to 84.

It is possible, and somewhat less unlikely, that his passing will one day be as far from the present day as my mother's is from me now. That would mean I make it to 70. And how often do I now think of my mother? What do I even remember of her? Does her death still affect me?

It does. It all does. Whether you realize it or not.

Everything matters.

Please, when I die, do not memorialize me. Do not leave for me a headstone. Do not spend money preserving my physical form in any way.

Take whatever money I have, and distribute it to charities, as you best see fit. Take whatever parts on my body you can use, give them to people who might still need them, and feed the rest to the dogs.

Really, I won't be offended.

I mean, I won't be anything at all. That's how it works.

But then, this.

It is two months After. Or maybe 10 years. Or it happened yesterday. Maybe All of the Above. I'm at Yankee Stadium again, at Heritage Field, the park where the old stadium used to be, now repurposed into a field of dreams for new generations to enjoy.

It is cold, but not unseasonably so. Sunny, blustery. Some white patches of the month's early snowstorm still dot the field.

In my jacket pocket, I have a clear Ziploc bag which holds about an 1/8th of ashes. Maybe a ¼. An 1/8th if you're, like, friends with the dealer. A fat 1/8th of Dad. Primo shit.

I can't be the first, or the 50th, person who has done this.

The only thing unique about your grief is that you experience it in the first person.

There is no one around, fortunately, and the gate to the field has been left open.

It's not a coincidence. It's just something that happened.

On a map back by the park's entrance, they have an outline showing exactly where the old field once lay. Home plate was somewhere in the shallow outfield of this new park, behind second base.

I look around, but there's no one close enough to know or care what I'm about to do. I crouch down, and open the bag. I pour the majority of its contents into my open palm, and rub the coarse, gravely pieces of him between my fingers.

I can't even see what I'm doing anymore.

I look into the middle distance, where a 4 train rumbles past. I look into the sky, where there is no Divine Being, since things don't exist just because we want them to.

"I'm sorry," I say. "I don't exactly know for what, but it feels like I should be, so I am. I'm doing ok. *I'm ok*! I'm still here. Irene's doing alright. We see each other more now. The dog's still good. I don't know how, but she is. I wish we –"

But I stop. Because I don't know what I wish. We do things, and we don't do things, and then one day, we can't do things anymore. If he had been a different person, and I had been a different person, then, well –

>No. That's not how Life works.

But also, not even that.

Because the reality is that I went to Heritage Field three weeks after he died and watched some kids playing football on a warm October afternoon. And I thought then that I would come back when I got his ashes. But his wife still hasn't picked them up from the morgue. And it's not like there's any urgency in that regard.

He's not going anywhere.

When I get those ashes, though, really, I'm going to try to spread them there, on that field. This is sincerely something I am going to try to do. I mean it. It truly, undeniably, might happen.

But the field might be locked when I go. Or in use. Or a security guard may see what I'm trying to do and stop me from holding my memorial services.

It is so, so hard to get a Hollywood ending.

And every day, from here on out, there will be something I would like to have told him. Or a link I would like to have sent him. Something I know he would have found funny. Or infuriating. Or both.

At the very least, we were pretty decent pen pals.

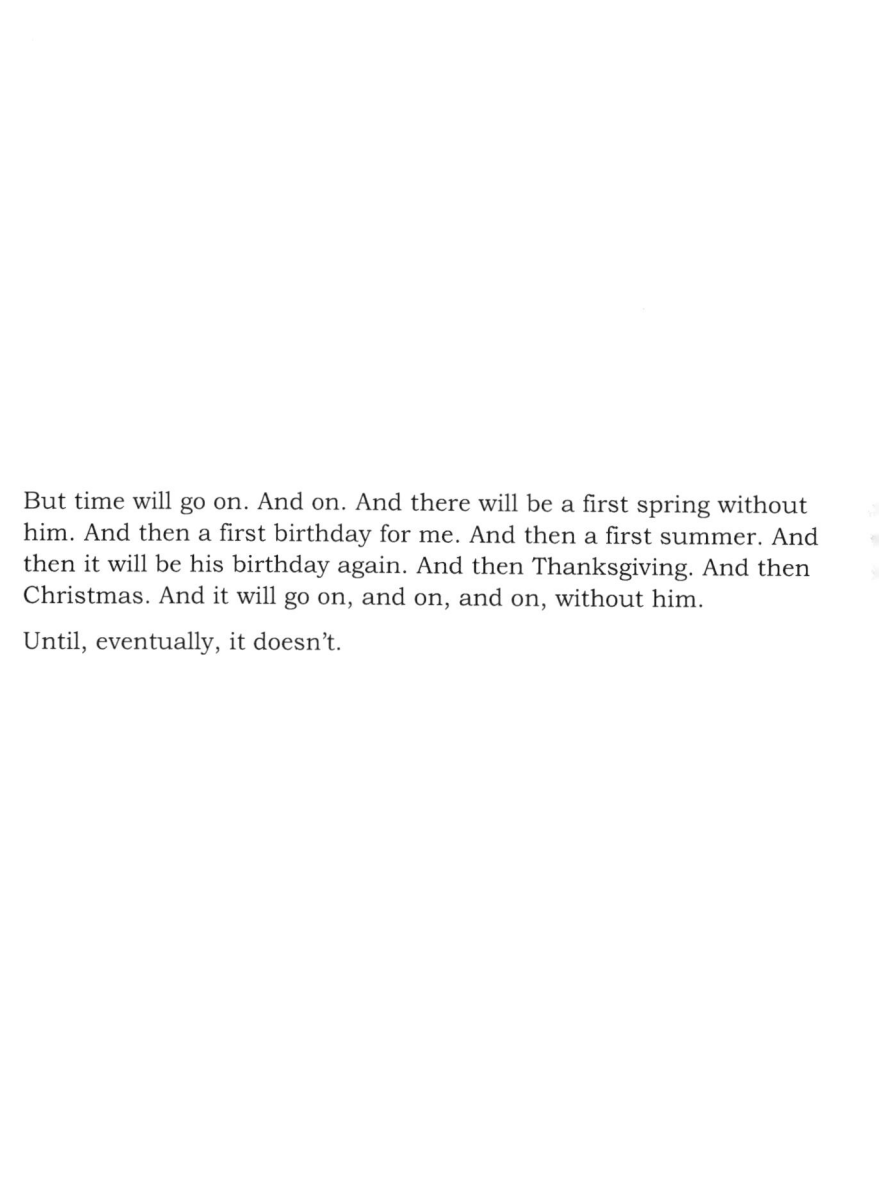

But time will go on. And on. And there will be a first spring without him. And then a first birthday for me. And then a first summer. And then it will be his birthday again. And then Thanksgiving. And then Christmas. And it will go on, and on, and on, without him.

Until, eventually, it doesn't.

There are days now, in the After, where I feel not measurably different than I did Before.

The literal hole in my heart I was born with closed slowly, over time. Perhaps the emotional one will, too.

But it's always going to feel a little empty in there.

You never really stop grieving.

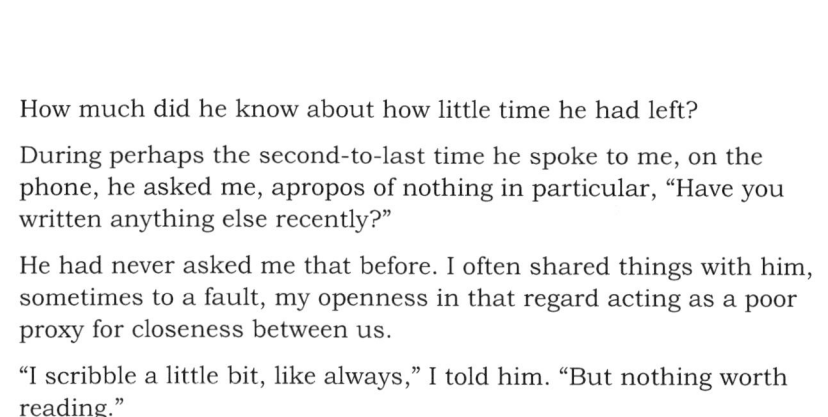

How much did he know about how little time he had left?

During perhaps the second-to-last time he spoke to me, on the phone, he asked me, apropos of nothing in particular, "Have you written anything else recently?"

He had never asked me that before. I often shared things with him, sometimes to a fault, my openness in that regard acting as a poor proxy for closeness between us.

"I scribble a little bit, like always," I told him. "But nothing worth reading."

Except, maybe, This.

Bryan Fox is still here. His father, Ross, is not. That hurts sometimes. But it's getting better.

Made in the USA
Middletown, DE
24 November 2019